Nehemiah in the Nineties

by

Mark Tolec

Grosvenor House
Publishing Limited

All rights reserved
Copyright © Mark Tolec, 2021

The right of Mark Tolec to be identified as the author of this
work has been asserted in accordance with Section 78
of the Copyright, Designs and Patents Act 1988

The book cover is copyright to Mark Tolec

This book is published by
Grosvenor House Publishing Ltd
Link House
140 The Broadway, Tolworth, Surrey, KT6 7HT.
www.grosvenorhousepublishing.co.uk

This book is sold subject to the conditions that it shall not, by way of
trade or otherwise, be lent, resold, hired out or otherwise circulated
without the author's or publisher's prior consent in any form of binding or
cover other than that in which it is published and
without a similar condition including this condition being imposed
on the subsequent purchaser.

A CIP record for this book
is available from the British Library

ISBN 978-1-83975-447-0

To John and Jane

The best parents I ever had

Contents

Prologue	Not Showing Fear	vii
Foreword		xiii
Acknowledgements		xix
Chapter 1	Beginnings	1
Chapter 2	New Life	15
Chapter 3	Sandhurst	37
Chapter 4	The Engineer Regiment	65
Chapter 5	The Escape from Las Vegas	79
Chapter 6	Learning to Build…The Troop Commanders' Course	87
Chapter 7	Welcome to Germany	105
Chapter 8	Germany Life and Lifestyle	119
Chapter 9	Pre-Bosnia, the Warm Up	141
Chapter 10	Deployed to Bosnia	155
Chapter 11	Specific Prayer	171
Chapter 12	The Rather Expensive Sentry Post	177
Chapter 13	When it is Time to Leave	185
Chapter 14	Overbridge	201
Chapter 15	The Underbridge and a Spot of Leave	207
Chapter 16	Home and Well	219
Glossary	British Army and Royal Engineer terms	229

Prologue - Not Showing Fear

2 Timothy 1:7:
'For the Spirit God gave us does not make us timid, but gives us power, love and self-discipline.'

In life, it is generally wise to not show fear and I learnt this in a very stark way when I visited South Africa in the early 90's.

Fear is an emotion that can have a great influence on the life of a Christian. It is a big subject which can fill many books, but I want to share how I learnt a lesson in not showing fear. In terms of interaction with people, showing fear can have unforeseen consequences. People who train animals will testify to this. When learning to ride a horse I soon found that it knew when I was scared or not and behaved accordingly. Once I had gripped my fear of falling off, I was well on the way to mastering the horse because it could no longer sense me being afraid. I believe this has parallels with people, too.

The Bible quotation above reassures Christians that these attributes of Jesus are alive in us through His Holy Spirit. I know it is easy to forget sometimes, and I am sorry to say that there are occasions when I have. But power, love and self-discipline are ours by right when we ask Jesus into our lives to live His life through us. And when we follow the prompting of the Holy Spirit, these attributes can come the fore.

The early 90s was an exciting time in world history for many reasons, one of which was that South Africa was at the transition between apartheid and democratic rule. And that is exactly where I found myself.

South Africa is an amazing place and it was difficult to not be affected by a country where so many people and ethnic groups believe they have a right to it. I met Zulus, Xhosa, Afrikaners, Asians and English-speaking white South Africans all of whom had a different perspective on their heritage and their land. What they all had in common was a passion for their stake in their South Africa.

So, there I was, in South Africa. I had driven from Johannesburg to visit a distant cousin whilst touring the region of south east South Africa called KwaZulu Natal.

My cousin had taken me to the Zulu War sites of Rourke's Drift (epic scene of British Army and Zulu bravery) and the very moving battlefield of Isandlwana. Before we set out, I remember he called his friend the local Police Commissioner, to check that the route was safe. Back came the reply:

'Yis, it should be fine; we hev not had a murder along thet road for over a week now!'

I decided to break up my journey from my cousin's farm back to Johannesburg (South Africa is a big place) and I had stopped for one evening in a small South African town between Durban and Jo'burg. I booked into a hotel and being of inquisitive disposition, I thought I would go and have a look around the town.

As I later learned and should have known already, this is not a wise thing to do in South Africa, but despite it being dark the town was well lit. It looked quiet enough to me. It was about 10 pm and I was the only one looking at the buildings and enjoying the ambience in the town square.

I thought I had the place to myself and was just heading back to the hotel when around a corner came a group of lively young black South African men. They were in high spirits and it looked like they had been drinking. Like similar groups of young men, the world over, they were jostling and laughing with one another as they went on their way. But when they saw me, on my own, they all fell silent and as one man started walking towards me.

I was now in great danger and I knew it. I should have been tucked up in bed and not out being a tourist at that late hour, on my own with no means of contact (this was before mobile phones). I remember being so suddenly frightened that it felt like an icy hand clutching my heart and insides. Things were not looking good, but within me I heard a still, small voice which I knew then and know now was the Holy Spirit. The voice said, *'Do not show fear.'*

Despite my pounding heart and every natural instinct within me urging me to flee like a gazelle, I mastered my emotions by heeding His voice, getting a grip and showing no fear.

Instead, I started walking towards the group in as relaxed manner as I could. This clearly surprised them, but the group still continued to walk towards me. The young men remained quiet, but now with one or two puzzled expressions; I suppose they were expecting me to run or at least look bothered.

When the gap between us had closed to twenty yards I made eye contact with as many of them as possible. I then took a quiet deep breath, smiled, raised my right hand in greeting and said in my most cheerful, warm and upbeat tone 'Good evening fellas, how's it going?'

The effect was amazing. It was as if I had slapped all the group in the face at the same time. They all looked so surprised and started to look at one another… but they kept walking and so did I.

I walked right through the group, smiling as genuinely as I could as I did so. Faithful to the Holy Spirit's command, I still resisted the temptation to sprint to what I hoped was safety. Instead, I kept my walk steady and measured. I did not turn my head or look back.

About ten seconds later I heard a furious discussion break out amongst the group in a language that was probably Zulu.

Then I heard a pair of running feet coming after me. With hindsight, I am glad that I did not bolt in panic at that point, but instead kept on walking at the same pace in the same direction as before.

The runner was one of the youths, clearly the gang leader. He ran past me and stopped dead in front of me. With a serious, earnest expression he faced me and held out his left-hand palm first and stopped me in my tracks by placing that hand on my chest.

He then held out his right hand, grasped my right hand, looked me in the eye, smiled and said in broken English:

'You ah de furst white man to greet me on de street in South Africa. It gives me great hope for de future of my country!'

He shook my hand again, smiling and laughing, then ran past me to re-join his mates. Waving to me, they carried on walking in their direction and I carried on walking in mine.

It was not the time to point out that I was a British tourist who should not have been there, but I can honestly say that he and his gang had met a Christian on the street who truly saw him and his friends as fellow human beings and not slaves. Even writing this story down now over 20 years later still gives me goose bumps. I often wonder what became of the gang leader and his gang, but I trust they are doing well and being a blessing to their country.

Had I shown fear that night in South Africa I am certain I would have become another South African mugging victim, or worse. Instead, the voice of the Lord turned the likelihood of a crime into an opportunity for encouragement and healing. The voice of the Lord brings positive change when He speaks to us and through us. In our everyday lives, are we listening to what He says and then doing it?

For me, if ever there was a good lesson of not showing fear and ruling the emotions, that was it. It is a strong reminder to do what the Lord is saying when he says it; when fear comes knocking at the door of our lives, sending faith to answer will mean there is no-one there.

And fear does come knocking.

The book of Hebrews says the Lord does not delight in him who shrinks back and it is so easy to allow fear to take root in our lives. I wish I could say I have applied that lesson perfectly 100% since then; I know there are times when I have failed to do so. But there are more times when the Lord has enabled me to succeed!

And He will do the same for you.

Foreword

I have written this book as a record of the Lord's goodness to me in the life He has called me to lead. This is a book which is intended to encourage men and women of God.

The book explains my decision to follow Christ, and my first few years as a Christian, as I worked out my walk with the Lord.

The Lord blessed me with great travel opportunities and some years of military service, so I had a wealth of different interesting scenarios in which to grow in my faith in Jesus.

I hope this book is entertaining, too and I trust that many of the incidents within these pages at least make the reader smile. Those affecting me actually happened and other stories I relate I have no reason to doubt. Take that as you will! Some of the incidents may not be commonly found within the pages of a book targeted at a Christian audience. I make no apology about that, because to omit them leaves out an essential humorous silver thread that runs through my military service. Given the range of creative characters that I encountered during my service with the British Army in general and the Royal Engineers in particular, these pages do contain a few anecdotes which should not really be part of a Sunday sermon. Yet they illustrate real life and over-editing them would rob some of the reality from these pages. Believe me, there are many incidents I have not included because they would not be appropriate for what is an ostensibly Christian book!

I have described situations that I have faced in my early Christian life; I have tried to be as honest as possible, changing or omitting names of people and places to give anonymity as appropriate. I have no desire to score points or embarrass anyone with this book. If I have mentioned names, it has been because I have considered it safe and appropriate to do so. Where I have not, it has been to save the person embarrassment. The book is not about singling out individuals; it is about showing that the Lord watches over those who follow Him, even when they do not realise it.

There is always the risk that my memory is not 100% accurate, but to the best of my knowledge all of what I have written is as true as I can recollect. Any errors are of course my own.

I have deliberately written to avoid jargon and with the assumption that readers will be unfamiliar with the military as a whole. I have tried to explain things simply and included a glossary to make it easier. I trust it is not too complicated and nor is it viewed as being patronising by anyone familiar with the military method and mindset.

The Lord gave me a very interesting few years as a commissioned officer in the British Army's Corps of Royal Engineers. I had a range of roles and experiences, through which the Lord guided and protected me. As I look back over twenty years later, I realise how much His hand was on me; I don't think I realised this fully at the time. There were many challenges to overcome, and despite being a while ago, I am strongly persuaded that they have parallels to those faced by Christians today.

I believe the Lord has placed this on my heart, to write about my years of service as a Royal Engineer officer because they are part of my years of service to the Lord Jesus, and formative ones, too. If sharing these experiences builds faith in Jesus;

fellowship with the Holy Spirit; love of the Bible and the God of the Bible amongst the Lord's people, then it will have achieved its purpose.

My prayer is that this book encourages and strengthens those who are serious about following the call of Jesus on their lives.

The Lord called me to the Army at an interesting time in history; the early nineties. This was just after the Berlin Wall had come down, and the consequent collapse of the Eastern Bloc. This led to the re-unification of Germany and huge changes to post-war Europe, the effects of which continue to be felt today despite major historic events since then.

It was also just after the first Gulf War against Saddam Hussein's invasion of Kuwait in 1990.

It was the decade where Yugoslavia entered the headlines as it tore itself apart through civil war, when Hong Kong was returned to China and when the government again began to reduce the size of the British Army.

But it was also the decade before 9/11 and the so-called war on terror. The word 'terrorist', at least in the UK, did not mean Islamic extremists, but referred mainly to the Irish Republican Army (IRA) in Northern Ireland, against which the British Army had been on operations in support of the Royal Ulster Constabulary (the police in Northern Ireland) since the early seventies.

Margaret Thatcher, then John Major, then Tony Blair, were the UK Prime Ministers. Bill Clinton was the main US President and the Soviet Union was breaking up into its component countries. The world was coming to terms with the end of the cold war and had perhaps not fully understood the growing international instability that would result.

It was the decade that 'Braveheart' and 'Titanic' were released, and I drove a brand-new Peugeot 306.

Rave was the new music, and the whole 'club' scene was beginning to emerge. We did still talk about discos though. Artists like 'The Spice Girls' were in the charts and Belinda Carlisle was selling albums, not doing cookery programmes. Many of today's pop artists were probably not born! We listened to records, but mainly tapes and it was the dawn of CDs.

The internet and emails were coming into common use by the end of the decade but were virtually unknown in the early nineties. Paperwork was either sent by post, or by fax machine. There was no such thing as social media; we used pay phones or landline, or we wrote letters. By the mid-nineties, mobile phones were becoming popular, having started as the size of house bricks, they gradually reduced to the dimensions we would recognise today. The hand-held touch screen was still the stuff of science fiction.

For the British Army, the decade marked a point in time. The end of the cold war meant that the long anticipated 'conventional' war in Europe was no longer expected to happen and the British Army undertook 'peace-keeping' operations throughout the nineties instead. The Twin Towers event in the next decade led to the British Army having to revert to much higher intensity operations than the 'peacekeeping' operations of the nineties, particularly in Afghanistan and Iraq. So, the nineties were a unique period of time and for me, it marked my years when my first proper full-time job was to be a regular British Army officer.

The backdrop to much of this narrative is my serving as part of the Royal Engineers, of which I am still extremely proud to have been an officer. The Lord called me to serve alongside a fantastic group of sappers, SNCOs and officers. I may not have got along with absolutely everyone, but most I found to be professional, loyal, good company whom I would trust implicitly in any situation. I hope my sincere respect and affection for those who served and still serve in the Royal Engineers also shows through this book.

Throughout my Christian life, I have been repeatedly inspired by the incredible story of Nehemiah, in the Old Testament, which resonates with my Royal Engineer background. In particular, the aspect of the story where he and his committed team are rebuilding the Jerusalem's fallen gates and walls. They are under constant threat of ambush and attack from their enemies, so they work together with weapons at hand and sentries posted. This sounds very similar to the combat engineering role of the Royal Engineers, where you are at constant readiness to revert to fighting as a normal soldier, in the midst of completing a sapper battlefield construction task.

I admire Nehemiah's determination, passion and sense of purpose and believe he would have found common ground with the Royal Engineers and their mottos... ubique (everywhere) and quo fas et gloria ducunt (where right and glory lead).

But through all of that, this book is fundamentally a testimony of the Lord's goodness and faithfulness to me, which I believe He wants me to share to encourage others in their journey with Him.

Acknowledgements

A book like this is certainly no individual effort and there are a number of people who have helped and encouraged me practically to write it. Unlike many authors, I have decided to preserve anonymity as much as possible; fame is not always the blessing we think it could be. I apologise to anyone who was expecting a more explicit mention.

Firstly, I would like to thank the Lord, about whom I trust this book faithfully testifies. He has kept me firmly in His Hand since he first saved me and continues to do so to this day, and I confidently expect Him to continue to do so. He is so good.

I would also like to thank my wife, for her patience, encouragement and advice with the drafts, which I think I accepted graciously. My three children, for whom some of these stories are perhaps too familiar, have helped to inspire me to write this all down.

I am very grateful to David P at church, for excellent constructive criticism that has enabled me to produce a better structured work than the manuscript I sent him. Also, to Nick S, one of my best friends who has given me such a sensible steer me to help me get the military Christian balance right. And to Lee D and Kath D, who brought a different military Christian flavour to these pages. Also, to Roger A at church, whose advice got me started.

My thanks to Rhett Parkinson and Val Hall, leading staff members at the Armed Forces' Christian Union who brought a good perspective and sensible edits. Val in particular helped with the readability of the text and its relevance to Christians in the military. I am also grateful to Val for the endorsement on the back cover. And thanks to Dan C for an outstanding cover design.

Also, to the Institution of Royal Engineers and Royal Engineers' Association, which responded to my invitation to read the final draft before publication and have raised no objections; I am glad to honour these excellent organisations in this way.

Finally, I wish to dedicate this book to my parents, both of whom continue to fight the good fight.

To my Dad, who imparted to me his love and fascination of all things military. And the Royal Engineers in particular.

And to my Mum, keeping cancer at bay and whose love of words and people remains with me to this day.

Mark Tolec[*]
South Wales, UK
December 2020

---

[*]Mark Tolec is a Pseudonym. The author wishes to glorify Jesus' name and not his own.

Chapter 1 - Beginnings

Proverbs 16:9:

'The heart of man plans his way, but the Lord establishes his steps.'

When I set out to join the British Army as an unsaved teenager, in my heart I was planning my way, but now I realise that all the time the Lord was establishing my steps for His purposes and my blessing.

Not every element of soldiering and being an army officer came naturally to me, but I worship a supernatural God and that changed everything.

This means growing in confidence that the Lord is for you, not against you.

This means believing that the Lord's sovereign purposes cannot be thwarted and that a Christian is secure in the Lord's purposes.

This means cheerfully acknowledging that the Bible is the Word of God and represents reality; miracles and incredible stories are the norm in the Bible, so we must expect them to be the norm for a Christian in their daily walk with the Lord.

And so the purpose of this book is to encourage Christians in their walk with the Lord.

* * * * *

I grew up in a fairly normal home in south west England. My Dad worked full time as a civil engineer for the Department of Transport and my Mum was a full-time mum because she and my Dad believed it was a better investment for our family. Mum was an English teacher by profession, but by the time my brother and I had reached comprehensive school age, she was happily immersed in village life. The Village Hall committee, parish magazine, village drama group and the Women's' Institute successfully erased any desire for her to return to teaching. I have a younger brother, who knows me well and with whom I am good friends, too.

I was not brought up in a completely Christian home because my Mum was a devout Catholic and my father was an agnostic. However, both my parents had, and still have, strong family values and so I was raised as a Roman Catholic because it was deemed by my parents to be a morally appropriate thing to do. My Dad could be very scathing about catholic values but was not sufficiently persuaded by Anglicanism to challenge my Mum's desire for my brother and I to be raised as Roman Catholics.

This meant I grew up only knowing about God through what I heard at Mass, but I was ignorant about the possibility of actually knowing him personally. I seldom, if ever, read the Bible.

I went to Mass every Sunday, and could recite all the words on the outside, but was so unaware of the personal relationship I could have with God on the inside. And this spiritual state of affairs persisted through my A levels and on into University, where we will resume this testimony tale.

From a very early age I had wanted to be an officer in the UK Armed Forces. My brother ended up as an officer in the RAF, possibly because my family went to a lot of RAF air shows when I was a lad, so the obvious choice was for me to aspire to be a fast jet pilot in the RAF. However, because I am quite colour-blind this was not going to happen. My colour-blindness became apparent to me as a teenager, which explained why school science lesson chemistry reactions were hard to spot (and why my taste in shirts is loud, not trendy). I began to look for other opportunities to be a military leader.

My Dad had been a Territorial Army (TA) officer throughout his working life. The TA (now the Army Reserve) was the part of the UK's Reserve Forces that trained civilians in their spare time to augment the efforts of the regular army in fighting off a potential invader. Back then in the eighties, the communist Soviet Union was very much alive and kicking, the Berlin Wall had not come down and the big threat to national security was the uneagerly anticipated invasion of Western Europe by the Armed Forces of the Warsaw Pact (the Soviet Union, Poland, East Germany, etc.).

The UK had a lead role in the North Atlantic Treaty Organisation (NATO) and the defence of Western Europe, with large numbers of British Army units based in Germany to repel the invader where he was first expected to strike. Such a war was expected to be of high intensity. At the time, many unit personnel based in Germany joked grimly about their life expectancy being measured in hours, not days or weeks, should the Soviet Bloc choose to cross the inner German Border.

One of the key roles of the TA was to provide a core of trained battle casualty replacements to quickly reinforce the regular army in the event of this Armageddon breaking out. These replacements ranged from specially trained individuals to whole battalions of infantry. The hallmark of the TA was that it comprised civilians who gave up weekends, evenings and a fortnight a year to train as soldiers and officers. There was always unhelpful speculation about the combat effectiveness of the TA, ranging from 'Little better than a drunken Dad's Army' to 'One cannot spot the difference between the TA soldier and the Regular soldier'. I will not add to the discussion because I am naturally biased about this issue, but I was always impressed by how good and dedicated Britain's part-time Army was, given its limited training resources.

So, my brother and I observed our Dad commuting to his day job in the Department of Transport regional office without much excitement and contrasted this sharply with his evident enthusiasm as the next TA weekend approached. It was clear that he had far more fun at weekends doing his soldiering as a TA officer with the Royal Engineers then ever he did in his day job. He would love his weekends away with his soldiers, repairing airfields, or shooting, or building bridges and I began to wonder if doing full-time, what my dad enjoyed so much part-time, might be the better career path for me.

I was also finding that Dad's military friends that I met were always more fun to be with than Dad's work friends. These soldiers and officers had a lively sense of fun and were quite respectfully rude, which is very attractive to a teenage boy (and I suppose to a boy of any age!). These men had travelled, they had seen things and had interesting, shared life experiences through being in the military. And there is no other word for it, they were manly. Again, I must stress that the sense of humour was so attractive and so funny. My Mum would always smile politely at the jokes of our civilian friends, but our military friends always made her laugh out loud and giggle. It just seemed that people in the British Army knew how to enjoy life and do so as a team. And so it began to exert quite a draw on me.

When as a 15-year-old in a comprehensive secondary in the south-west of England, I was asked what I wanted to do when

I left school, I was reasonably sure that I wanted to be a regular, full time officer in the Royal Engineers. This raised a few eyebrows at the time, because the rest of my pals who wanted to join the Armed Forces had no intention of becoming officers! However, the south-west of England is a good recruiting ground for the Armed Forces, and I was generally encouraged.

No other career options appealed to me, and the UK economy in the late eighties was not offering many long-term jobs, either.

Another factor which influenced me was the British Forces' victory in the Falklands War in 1982. It is easy to forget the significance of the Falklands Conflict because it seems a while ago. The war held the nation in thrall because on a daily basis its progress was followed on TV in most people's living rooms. I believe it was the first UK 'foreign war' that had been watched on TV. Unlike the American equivalent of Vietnam, a decade or so earlier, the Falklands War only lasted a few months. Also, generally speaking, it enjoyed popular support and ended with a victory for the home nation. The shorter duration of the Falklands War meant that there were less casualties too. I realise this to be a gross oversimplification, but I would ask the reader to see this from the perspective of a teenage boy, rather than it being a profound comment on either conflict.

The fighting quality of the British Forces became apparent throughout the Falklands War, especially when they overcame numerically superior Argentine forces. The recurring message was that the UK Armed Forces were an elite organisation. This 'Falklands Factor' meant that the stock of the UK Armed Forces rode very high across the country throughout the eighties. Living in the South West of England, with so many Royal Navy and Royal Marines units based nearby which had played such a role in the 1982 victory, we were never far from this patriotic military positivity.

Meanwhile, I grew into a rural teenager loving the outdoors, hillwalking, wildlife, military history, socialising etc. Socialising was a laugh once I had passed the age of 16 and could get away with being served beer in my hometown's pubs, so I developed quite a taste for ale and the lively high jinks that go with it. I was starting to learn about girls, too, yet I must acknowledge that my Roman Catholic fear of an angry God kept me from ladies' beds and consequently out a lot of trouble. It didn't feel like it at the time, because I seemed to be missing a lot of fun, but looking back I would have got into all sorts of bother. The Lord does indeed establish the steps.

However, in sixth form college where I studied Advanced Levels before selecting which degree to do, I struggled academically with my chosen subjects of Chemistry, Physics and Maths. I had taken these options because they seemed to align with my choice of career. In hindsight, this was a big mistake, however commendable my motives. I have since learnt that it is always better to choose subject options that you are passionate about, rather than those that might be of use. Consequently, a person's career direction is more likely to be something that is of interest, instead of something to just pay the bills. The national economic outlook was poor from where I saw it and I did not want to be another out-of-work history graduate, but today I spend much more of my spare time reading about history than ever I do on engineering! Despite all this, I did work hard, and was predicted to get grades C in each of these three subjects.

The next question was where I was going to study. I may have been under eighteen, but I realised that the location of my university was important. I also knew that I had a great opportunity to acquire life experience, so the safe option of studying in the south west at either Bristol, Exeter or Plymouth was just that...safe. I looked north (the cost of living in London was very high, even then) and picked some likely cities. I reckoned that the civil engineering departments in each university were very similar.

After five visits, I had one clear favourite: Newcastle-Upon-Tyne. How do I describe the impact of that overnight familiarisation visit to Newcastle to view the university and enjoy a preview of student life? It was over 300 miles from my hometown and a universe apart. The locals spoke with the most incredible Geordie dialect, so different to the 'ooh-arr' farmer accents with which I had grown up in south west England. It was a huge urban sprawl that had really suffered during the recession of the seventies and early eighties, yet was accelerating out of this with a contagious, cheerful optimism. The city had just opened Eldon Square, and the Metro Centre lay nearby; both enormous shopping centres. Newcastle even had its own metro, imaginatively called the Metro.

Just beyond the city was the stunning Northumbrian Coast, with the deserted splendour of the Cheviot Hills within reach as well. So I was adamant that I was going to Newcastle University to study civil engineering and so Newcastle became my number one option following the familiarization visit I had made.

However, my hard work was not enough to overcome a lack of ability and aptitude for Maths, Physics and Chemistry. Opening the envelope on A level results day left me crushed, but not altogether shocked, when I ended up with two D's and an N. These are hardly ideal grades with which to design bridges and impress academics.

As a Christian, we have no choice but to believe that our lives are in the Lord's hands. This is put to the test on exam results days, especially if the results are a disappointment and mean that the expected next step is now not going to happen. As a non-Christian, unaware that the Lord directs the steps, to me this drama had now become a crisis.

Thankfully the army and other sensible employees do not just look at a student's academic ability. Whilst at sixth form I had chosen to join the Territorial Army as a private soldier to have some experience of life in the ranks before going on to become an officer. Incidentally, for years afterwards I drew on this experience to help me understand the men I was aspiring to lead. If nothing else, it taught me how *not* to be an officer.

The officer is always keenly observed by soldiers and as a TA private soldier in the TA Royal Engineers (called a Sapper), I saw how things like cynicism and unprofessionalism on the part of an officer, however minor, was always noted by the sappers. I also learned that sappers were not stupid and were keen to be led; they were less keen to be driven. But more of that later, the point is that my being already in the TA before the end of my A levels helped me when I crashed and burned with my results.

I think most of us from the UK can easily recollect *that* August day when we received our A level or GCSE exam results, knowing how it can affect our choice of career, university, workplace and consequently the rest of our lives. I am sure most of us can also recollect the actions we may have needed to take afterwards, whether it was a sigh of relief or implementing a rapid Plan B (or C or D) to prevent the next year being spent doing filler jobs that weren't even part of Plan Z.

My challenge was that I had fallen very short of the CCC 'A' level grades required by Newcastle University. With no university place, the Royal Engineers may have wanted to reconsider whether I was the type of officer they wanted. I had both the Royal Engineers to convince to sponsor me through University and the University to convince to take me on as a civil engineering undergraduate.

Holding my pathetic piece of paper from the exam board, with my weak grades standing for 'Donald Duck Nil' instead of 'Amazing Alpha Academic' (or even 'Chasing Civils Career', which would have seen me home and dry), I decided upon a strategy based on some crucial intelligence information I had just gleaned from one of my Dad's civil engineering magazines. For it just so happened that the year of my 'A' level results coincided with a national shortage of trained civil engineers.

I vividly recall phoning the Army on the home landline that August afternoon, with my heart thumping and my parents not quite out of earshot. When I was connected to the recruitment department, I strongly hinted my belief that that the University would accept me if the army did and that I had already joined the TA to learn about life as a soldier before becoming an officer. The official on the other end of the line was impressed.

I then rang the University admissions department and said that the Royal Engineers would accept me if the University did. That year the University was short of applicants for civil engineering. Of course, there was the national shortage of which I reminded them. And from the University's viewpoint an applicant going to the army after his studies was a safer bet that a random student with no need to stay. Thankfully, neither organisation went to the trouble of contacting each other to cross reference my story. The upshot was that both organisations said 'Yes!'. Crucial intelligence information plus some sensible groundwork as a private soldier in the Territorial Army had carried me through!

Looking back, my approach was hardly oozing with integrity, but there was some initiative there too and I had not yet given my life to Christ! And more importantly, the Lord wanted me in Newcastle, but I did not realise that at the time.

I spent the next three years studying civil engineering at the University of Newcastle Upon Tyne.

My first year was spent in weekends away with either the University Officers' Training Corps (OTC) or the University Caving Club, interspersed with some frantic studying to keep up with my Civil Engineering Course. These weekends were very intensive and would usually feature drinking before, during and after any activities. Sometimes drinking was the activity, especially if the caves were flooded because of heavy rain or the OTC training had finished early.

With the OTC, many hours were spent marching over the Pennine hills of Northern England. Then next weekend, with the University Caving Club, many hours were spent crawling under those same Pennine hills instead. They were fun times.

The OTC were a high-spirited lot who enjoyed life and I found that I fitted in quite well with the military crack and banter. My joining the TA as a private soldier had given me some street-cred amongst my fellow students, though one of the sergeant majors reckoned it was because I had better pay rates as a TA soldier (he was right – I did!).

One of the advantages of being in the TA Royal Engineers (as well as the OTC) was the opportunity to serve with a TA engineer unit and I took the opportunity to do so. Back then, some TA units only required its soldiers to serve a minimum of two weekends and a fortnight 'annual camp' each year, though many soldiers did more weekends and camps. I took advantage of this situation to improve my understanding of military life, and the foundations of being a sapper, which is a private soldier in the Royal Engineers.

I learned first-hand how important it was for officers to behave well in public and in private, and that they had no need to talk down to their soldiers. I learned how frustrating it was when an officer considered me to be stupid because I was a 'sapper', which made me consider carefully what sort of officer I was going to be. The knowledge that I was aspiring to be an officer one day provoked an interesting reaction from the JNCOs and SNCOs in my unit. Some were rude, or humorous about it, as you would expect, but a significant number drew me to one side and gave me nuggets of advice. Much of this followed the theme that I had two ears and one mouth, so as a new officer I should listen carefully to the advice I was given by JNCOs and SNCOs and not think I knew it all. They would point out some of the officers in our unit who came across as thinking they knew it all, and I realised that this was wise counsel if I were to be an effective sapper officer and not turn out like that.

Indeed, for any Christian in the workplace, particularly in any form of leadership, arrogance, hubris and pride are not virtues. These traits may act as a comfort blanket for the Christian leader, but they risk alienating them in their role, and mean the team follows only because it has to comply, instead of because it wants to comply. We only need to see Jesus, who is clear about his identity, yet identifies equally with the Samaritan woman, the blind beggar, the humble Pharisee and the Roman centurion. No arrogant pride there.

So, my time with the part time army of the UK was not wasted and in fact led to some great learning opportunities. For example, I learned to build equipment bridges (Bailey Bridge) by actually being part of the sapper workforce who built it. This was to come in very useful later on in my life.

Another one of these learning opportunities was a fortnight in Gibraltar, to help strip out an old pumping station. This was stimulating work and meant taking apart the machinery ready for the demolition itself. However, whilst scrambling atop a large, greasy piece of metalwork, I slipped and put my hand through a glass window, which then snagged on the shards. Let's just say the blood spurted out in time with my heartbeat and was a fascinating red fountain. My fellow sappers (who had not gone pale) wrapped and elevated my arm before bundling me off in a Land Rover to the hospital, where I received 12 stiches. So much for youthful enthusiasm.

However, the skin healed fast. So fast in fact, that the following week I took part in a bar game called 'the coffin'. This involved sitting in a box (the coffin), which is balanced on a horizontal wooden pole, which is supported at either end by a chair. The contestant first has to sit level in the coffin, using a broom handle for stability, before using the broom handle to knock off four beer mats placed on the end of four chairs just within reach. So far, so good. Alas, my sense of balance and coordination did not make me a champion, and out I tumbled, landing on my damaged hand. And I realised very quickly that it was not tomato sauce on the floor beneath me…my hand had 'burst'. The skin had healed, but the wound was deeper than anyone had realised, and a cavity had been unwittingly created when the wound had first been stitched up. So back I went to the hospital to something less than a hero's welcome, although being a military hospital there were plenty of staff there who saw the funny side of it.

All of this time as a private soldier, even as a part time sapper, was valuable experience for me. This may not have been much use in a civil engineering degree, but certainly gained me some unplanned street cred with my fellow students, especially in the OTC.

As a student, I did other activities outside my studies and the TA.

Caving club weekends were slightly different, featuring some hairy pieces of cave exploration for novices like me. Dressed in wetsuits wearing wellington boots, and carrying coiled ladders, helmets and lamps, we made a strange procession from the car park to the cave entrance. Cave entrances varied from enormous caverns like aircraft hangars to holes in the ground like a badger sett. Then into the cave proper, for between 6-10 hours. Caving varied. Sometimes it was just a long, cold wet, muddy crawl through a narrow tunnel, via a couple of cold sumps to really freeze you, before coming to a chamber the size of the living room that the guidebook said was the end of the system. Other times the final chamber would be the size of St Paul's Cathedral and on entering it I would feel like Samwise Gamgee in Lord of the Rings, on beholding the dwarf realm of Moriah for the first time.

The most exciting of these caving trips were when we would follow the course of a stream down under the mountains, using coiled metal ladders to climb down the waterfalls (or pitches) if necessary. These ladders were bolted to the cave wall and left in situ to be collected up on the return journey. On one such subterranean trip the leader had not checked the weather forecast before we went underground and it was only after a few hours that he realised that the volume of water in the stream was much greater than at the start of the trip. This was because the predicted torrential rain that weekend had only started just after we had gone into the cave system. I have never forgotten the hollow-eyed expression on his face as realisation dawned on him that we had to turn back and make for the surface immediately if we to avoid being cut off and potentially drowned by the rising water.

It was a desperate race against time and even I could see that the level was rising and the trickle of water in the pitches that we had descended were now raging torrents up through which we had to climb. It was with grim urgency that we toiled back up through a cave system that was filling quickly. Where we had walked down a tunnel, we swam and scrambled up a watercourse before the next vertical climb though a Niagara waterfall which marked the next pitch.

We all got out in time and of course being young and therefore immortal we counted it a great adventure. Later that weekend, I proudly recounted my exploits to my Mum during my weekly phone call, and she received them somewhat less enthusiastically. I learnt then that there were some adventures that required a decent time interval before sharing them with your Mother. This was a handy lesson for when I later visited Bosnia, Northern Ireland and other interesting places. And again, the Lord had His hand upon my life even before I had given it to Him.

However, I was not entirely convinced that the cave leader had learned his lesson and together with my reading the poor statistics of how few people returned from cave diving expeditions, I reckoned that caving was not going to be my number one hobby.

Now into my second year it was more studies and some more OTC weekends, but I throttled back on the caving trips! The course work was beginning to build up and so I had less opportunity to flit off on weekends than before.

This allowed other influences into my life…

Chapter 2 - New Life

Acts 2:37-39:

'When the people heard this, they were cut to the heart and said to Peter and the other apostles, 'Brothers, what shall we do?' Peter replied, 'Repent and be baptised, every one of you, in the name of Jesus Christ for the forgiveness of your sins. And you will receive the gift of the Holy Spirit. The promise is for you and your children and for all who are far off – for all whom the Lord our God will call.'

Meanwhile, I had noticed 'born-again' Christians when I was at Newcastle University and found many (but not all) of them to be boring and nerdy. Yet among them were Christians that I liked who were good fun to be with and not afraid to challenge my staunch Roman Catholicism.

At this point I considered myself to be a Christian and was quite condescending towards these born-again types who seemed to not take God seriously and have no sense of tradition. However, there was a Christian guy from Northern Ireland on my course, who did not fit my convenient stereotype and whose lively sense of fun together with his unshakeable integrity severely challenged my status quo. And he talked all the time about Jesus, not merely 'God', or 'the Good Lord', but Jesus. And this concept gnawed away at me, though I did not understand why it did so at the time.

The University Christian Union was organising an evangelism week and I thought I would go along and support, if only to encourage my well intentioned (if oddly informal) Christian friends.

A preacher called J John was in town and I went along to hear him. He was the main attraction for the evangelism week and was preaching in Jesmond Parish Church in Newcastle. I had even tried to persuade others to come along and hear him because I was convinced that I was a Christian already, even though my lifestyle of binge drinking, swearing, late nights out and miscellaneous pagan revelry as a student would have said otherwise.

I listened hard to this preacher as he vividly defined who Jesus Christ is and who He said He is. I had not heard Jesus described in this way. It was an electrifying message, but there were two significant revelations that changed my life forever:

- The first revelation was that Jesus did not have to go through that awful death on the cross. He could have opted out at any stage during his trial by simply saying He was not the Son of God. But He was, and is, the Son of God and He would not deny His identity. So, to the cross he went and then was resurrected on the third day.
- The second revelation was that this same Jesus was very much alive and well and genuinely wanted a relationship with me. As a Roman Catholic, I was aware of a distant God having some kind of care for mankind, but a personal relationship through Jesus Christ with the living God was a whole new concept to me.

My only response was to crumple as I realised that my sins could only be taken away by asking Jesus to do it through His blood. I remember saying to the Lord, that I now realised was up close and personal: *'Yes Lord, I'm a sinner. Please can you sort my life out? I'm sorry for my sins and you are now in charge of my life. I place it into your hands'.*

That changed everything.

I thought I would have to become a vicar and give up my life in the army. I thought I would no longer be able to have any fun. I was wrong.

In the days and weeks following my being born again, I started to read the Bible for the first time and to pray in expectation of hearing a response from the Lord. It was and is so exciting knowing that you can have a 1-1 with the creator of the universe and the guy who rose from the dead.

Very early on the Lord spoke to me saying that He still wanted me to become an Army officer in the Royal Engineers. I thought it was my plan, but all the time it had been His. The Lord made it very clear to me that He had no difficulty with me serving in the British Army as an officer. But He was very interested in what type of Army officer I would become. Would I behave as a Christian or hope that no-one found out I was a Christian?

For example, I now understood that a Christian Army officer does not murder innocent civilians or prisoners in times of conflict. I settled the issue of whether I could kill or not, through determining that it was lawful to kill, but not lawful to murder. After all, the Lord had given the Ten Commandments to His people before, not after the conquest of the Promised Land.

Settling the key question of 'is it lawful to kill?' is understandably important for military Christians. Not surprisingly, it is also important to settle this for the benefit of your fellow officers and the soldiers that you are to lead. They are very aware that hesitation or lack of resolution on the part of a Christian officer would jeopardize their safety and the success of any mission.

As for me, I was certain that I would not hesitate to shoot at anyone who was firing on me, my soldiers, unit or anyone I was duty bound to protect. Even if this meant me firing first to prevent subsequent enemy fire. This also meant I grasped the important role an officer has in inspiring strong adherence to the Geneva Convention and the Law of Armed Conflict, which are basically international rules which provide for the safety of prisoners, wounded, civilians, property etc. during time of war. All armed forces are supposed to abide by these rules, the sad reality is that throughout history this has not always been the case. A stark negative example of what can go wrong when an officer fails to lead headstrong soldiers is the My-Lai massacre in the Vietnam War.

So, I was clear that I could not and would not compromise my faith in Jesus, and that I would not hide it. I knew, and know, that one day I will face Him, and He will ask me questions about how I led my life. I chose to fear Him, and not what people might think of me.

I carried on with OTC, but gradually learned to curb the wild drinking because the morning after I no longer felt proud of myself. Instead I felt I had let down my best friend, which of course, I had. As I took hold of the new life that Jesus was giving me, my shallower friends drifted off; my good friends became even better ones. Much to the surprise of many, I found I was perfectly able to mess around and have fun whilst sober and did not need the Dutch Courage that I once did. In other words, Jesus did not strip me of my sense of fun and humour, but He started to refine it. This process is ongoing over twenty-five years later!

My parents wondered if I had joined a sect and I think for some years they were concerned about me. Perhaps they do still scratch their heads a little! I can only say that since giving my life to Jesus there is nothing I would wish to retain from my old life because I have the sure hope of eternity when I eventually pop my clogs. And in the meantime, I have the limitless resources of heaven to help me live life to the full right now. This sounds very simplistic, and life is not simple, but we must start somewhere.

As we saw before in the previous chapter, Proverbs 16:9 says 'The heart of man plans his way, but the Lord establishes his steps'.

I thought that I had got myself into Newcastle University, but now I can see the hand of the Lord on me before I had even acknowledged Him as Lord. I know the cynic would say it was all down to the luck of the draw, but I know different. The Lord is in control of a person's life and while unplanned and difficult things can happen in a person's life, we always have the hotline to God through Christ to intervene in circumstances. This is how I know that God has a plan for yours and my life, even before you know it.

The salvation experience goes beyond that of repenting of your sins and asking Jesus to be Lord of your life. There are the baptisms in water and of the Holy Spirit to be included too. I do not know how Christians manage their walk with the Lord without the old life being cut off, which is water baptism, and without the empowerment of Heaven which is the baptism of the Holy Spirit. In the New Testament, especially throughout the Book of Acts, it is clear that both baptisms are the norm for Christians.

I mentioned to one of my good Christian friends that as a new believer I was not sure if I needed baptism because I had been christened as a child. He smiled and produced a page of bible references to believer's baptism by full immersion. I got the picture.

Water baptism by full immersion does represent the public removal of a Christian's old life and means that your walk with the Lord is spiritually uncluttered. I understand that in areas of the world where the church is persecuted, the challenges for new Christians begin, not when they repent of their sins and call Jesus 'Lord', but once they are baptised. This is because baptism in water represents their old life ending for ever. The baptism waters are symbolised by the Red Sea cutting off the Israelites permanently from Egypt; there is no going back to your former life.

As 2 Corinthians 5:17 says:

> *'Therefore, if anyone is in Christ, he is a new creation; the old has gone; the new has come!'.*

Being filled with the Holy Spirit and speaking in tongues is so prevalent across the church of the New Testament I can find no evidence for it *not* being a hallmark of the Christian. And in simple terms, if the Lord is offering the same mighty power as that which raised Him from the dead, I struggle to understand why a Christian would not want to accept it in his or her life. After all, in John 10:10 Jesus says

> *'The thief comes only to steal and kill and destroy; I have come that they might have life and have it to the full.'*

This means Jesus' intention is for Christians to have a full life, which means being full of His Holy Spirit. Back in the nineties this was still a hot topic amongst Christians, with the two often opposing views of the evangelical 'no' and the charismatic 'yes' to speaking in tongues. I believe many more Christians now are open to the Holy Spirit, and I know that what I emphatically believe and advocate is that every Christian must speak in tongues. Why live the Christian life without the Holy Spirit?

Speaking in tongues was not something I had heard of before and it was only on visiting one of the 'modern' charismatic churches in Newcastle that I had any idea. I heard an electric sermon on it from one of the elders, describing how there is power in the name of Jesus to do the will of Jesus. This sounded very different to the sometimes cringing and apologetic Christianity that is often put forward as active faith, and I was inspired. I spoke to the elder about this after the meeting and he replied in his Geordie accent 'Well son, let's get you full of the Spirit laike'.

And he laid hands on me and I was filled with the Holy Spirit 'laike', immediately. My goodness did I feel the presence of the Lord. Powerfully He moved on me and left me in no doubt about the reality of being filled with His Holy Spirit and speaking in tongues. It was a powerful baptism experience which left me flat on my back in the church office, calling out my praises to the Lord as wave after wave of Holy Spirit power moved upon me. It was unforgettable and life changing for me.

It also meant that I had no rational explanation for what the Lord had done for me when He saved me. When I suddenly acquired a new language in line with the Word of God, it left me in no doubt that Jesus was real, the Bible was real, and my salvation was real. And that utter certainty has been an absolute bedrock to my faith and has left me incapable of denying Jesus because I remain so completely convinced of His present reality and His reality to come.

I was filled with the Holy Spirit in Bethshan Assemblies of God Church in Newcastle, baptised in water (full immersion) in Heaton Baptist Church, Newcastle and born again in Jesmond Parish Church, Newcastle. I had to learn about church hopping, it would appear, though this was quite normal among students at the time. And I was to find in the army that

I had to take fellowship as and when I could find it due to the highly nomadic lifestyle of HM Forces. A certain amount of church hopping was to become a way of life.

I concluded my second year at university in a very different spiritual state to how I had begun and was embarking on a very different life trajectory to what I had imagined less than a year before.

That summer I had been successful in getting a place as a 'venturer' on an Operation Raleigh expedition to Zimbabwe, so for ten weeks I was living under the stars doing a range of different projects in the African bush. It was amazing and the task ranged from trekking, to making an elephant fence, to canoeing across Lake Kariba, to building a medical clinic in the Eastern Highlands. It was a superb experience for a young man leaving his teens and starting his twenties. And I found that my time running a project to build the medical clinic went well; my sense of drive and urgency earned me the nick name 'Mark Chop-Chop' from the local villagers. I trust it was a compliment. I was certainly encouraged with the practical direction of my military career choice that the Lord had affirmed for me.

However, the real challenge for me was to maintain my integrity as a Christian alongside 100 or so other lively UK 'venturers' of my own age or thereabouts. They were the most delightful 'sinners' who worked hard, were great company, were high-spirited, drank beer and sang songs round the campfire, yet they took their clothes off for fun and engaged in many other activities forbidden to a Christian.

On day one, hour one, minute one of the expedition, I knew I had to get my Christian colours nailed to the mast or else it would have been very easy to have compromised who I am in Christ and then let Jesus down. Interestingly, non-Christians do expect a Christian to stand up for what he or she believes and so despite the inevitable idiots who have a problem with Christianity, I found I was accorded a degree of respect by the majority. I still sang funny songs, danced around the campfire and enjoyed life. But I absented myself from strip poker, naked wrestling and of course from striking up an inappropriate liaison with a non-believing girl. In short, I thoroughly enjoyed myself, but I did not sin. And that is what the Lord expects of us. We are not to live our lives under the bushel.

What is acceptable, and unacceptable, behaviour on an expedition like that is obvious to a Christian. I learned that the Lord really does honour the Christian that does not compromise. I had many conversations during those 10 weeks where I could share my testimony of what the Lord had done for me. Writing this is challenging me to get back in contact with some of these guys, to see where they are on their spiritual journey. Some of the tearaways back then are probably sober, respectable accountants or librarians now. I do hope some of them are now saved.

Another dimension to the expedition for me was experiencing that there really is power in the name of Jesus. Those were instances where I learned the power of the Lord in a situation.

The first two took place during the canoe expedition across Lake Kariba. The routine was to canoe for the morning, have a long lunch on the lake shore (or an island) and then canoe for part of the afternoon before setting up camp for the evening. During the lunch breaks, most of the venturers were happy to lounge and chill. I have a more inquisitive disposition than that, and so I would stroll off along the bank or into the bush to see what wildlife was around.

Usually, I would startle the odd zebra or gazelle. However, on one occasion as I sauntered along the lakeside, imagine my surprise when forty yards up the bank from me, a large rock suddenly rolled onto four short piggy legs and snorted at me... I had woken a dozing bull hippopotamus and I was standing between it and water. I must admit to my knees knocking together in fright as I realised my predicament. One does not put oneself between a bull hippo and water – they feel threatened and charge. And bull hippos weigh tonnes, can move quickly and have large tusks. They have no respect for an unarmed person and more people are killed by hippos in Africa then by any other large animal. I had no chance of winning a sumo contest with a bull hippo.

So you see my dilemma. I froze so's not to alarm it...and started speaking in tongues, quietly at first, then a little louder to drown out the sound of my heart thumping my ribcage. And the bull kept staring at me...then started to blink...then the blinks got longer...and then it sagged noisily back onto the ground again and went back to sleep. I stepped quietly backwards, retracing my steps, still speaking in tongues, but punctuating it with a few quiet cries of 'thank you' to the Lord.

I crept back to the rest of the venturers who were just starting to stir and just mentioned I had seen a hippo, rather than describing my near-death experience.

Not having learnt my lesson, a couple of days later at another lunch stop on one of the small lake islands about 500 metres across, I set off to see what was through the scrub on the far shore of the island. As I emerged through the bushes on the other side, I unwittingly trapped three elephants on a small spit of land; and they were not happy. Elephants fear man but are very defensive and my sudden appearance had spooked them. The largest was taking its role as 'leader' seriously and was exhibiting some interesting behaviour. I have always been interested in African wildlife and therefore I was aware that when an elephant gurgles, rolls up its trunk and flaps its ears, it is about to charge.

Sure enough, this elephant was gurgling, rolling up its trunk and flapping its ears. Not good.

And then from seemingly nowhere I was reminded of some teaching I had received earlier that year in church in Newcastle, the day I was filled with the Holy Spirit. That teaching was that the spiritual man has dominion over animals, not to abuse them, but to rule them in a godly way. Of course, it was the Lord talking to me at the very time that I needed Him to do so.

I immediately decided that in all good conscience I had not come to the island to harm the elephants. I had made a simple mistake, that's all, and the elephant had no right to charge me into a red pulp for it. So I spoke aloud to the elephant and said:

'In Jesus' name, cease rebellion. Do not harm me, I mean you no harm'.

Three seconds later the elephant stopped gurgling. It unrolled its trunk, stopped flapping its ears and started feeding quietly on the nearby vegetation. Once again, I back tracked carefully through the undergrowth and told my friends to not go through there because there were elephants feeding. And I told myself that next time I went for a lunchtime ramble, I was going to take a lot more care.

It is important that I insert a health warning at this point, lest the reader assume I spend my weekends vaulting into the lion enclosure at the local zoo, challenging the beasts therein to take me on. Let us be clear that the Lord rescued me from both events, where my unthinking actions got me into two tricky situations. The Lord, gracious as ever, also taught me something each time which has blessed me ever since and, I trust, blesses the reader too.

The final testimony of the power of God that I wish to share from my time in Zimbabwe is when a group of us venturers were invited to a village one evening. So far, so good. But little did I know what sort of evening it was.

We all gathered round a flat area in the middle of the village where some impressive tribal dancing was taking place. The Zimbabweans were superb dancers and this evening was no exception. It was very energetic, the groups swinging to the African rhythm, the women ululating in time with the beating drums and everyone just having one big African party.

Whereupon, entering at speed from stage right, the local witch doctor appeared. He was wearing an enormous African mask and was attended by three additional drummers. He immediately began to caper aggressively in the middle of the dancing area and it drew everyone's attention. It transformed the whole tempo and 'feel' of the evening; I immediately felt my skin crawl. Something was not right. Yet my fellow Operation Raleigh venturers were thoroughly enjoying the new spectacle. So what was wrong?

I was learning that the Lord shows spiritual people spiritual things and having been filled with the Holy Spirit, I was now much more attuned to spiritual things. Africans take spiritual matters very seriously, much more than westerners do. What my fellow venturers were enjoying as harmless fun, was in fact an occultic dance of demon worship. I did not fully understand this at the time, but I knew *in my spirit* that something was very adrift. And I sensed that that the Lord was not happy about it, either.

In the book of Ezekiel in the Old Testament, in chapter 22:30 it says:

> *'I looked for a man among them who would build up the wall and stand before me in the gap on behalf of the land so that I would not have to destroy it, but I found none'.*

The Lord is always looking for people who will be used by Him to intervene. I did not understand the theology of this at the time, but I knew that the witch doctor's demonic dancing was wrong and that something had to be done. So, quietly bowing my head and without drawing any attention to myself, I cried out to the Lord:

'Please stop this now Lord'.

I didn't know what I expected to happen…

Suddenly all three drummers stopped drumming simultaneously. The witch doctor stopped in mid-prance, like a freeze frame. All four then looked at each other quizzically, as if to say, 'I thought *you* said stop'. Finally, as one man, all three drummers picked up their drums and wandered off into the night. Five seconds later they were followed by a very bewildered looking witch doctor. The villagers, who had been getting very carried away by the witch doctor's intervention, seemed to have snapped out of a group trance and quietly made their way home. All the other Operation Raleigh venturers looked at each other, shrugged, and mooched back to our campsite.

The party was over because the Lord had ended it.

I hope these testimonies encourage the reader that a Christian is never alone. And that the power of God is there to see us through the valley of the shadow. I was to draw on this truth many times as a single man in the army...a Christian is never alone, because as Hebrews 13:5-6 says:

> '...because the Lord has said 'Never will I leave you, never will I forsake you'. So we say with confidence, 'The Lord is my helper; I will not be afraid. What can man do to me?'

My final year in Newcastle, not surprisingly, was consumed with preparations for final exams. I grew in the Lord, read the Bible in under a year and secured a 2:2 Civil Engineering Honours Degree by 0.2%; I must have over-revised!

Over the summer, I was privileged to secure a 3-week attachment in Hong Kong with the Queen's Ghurkha Engineers. That was very valuable experience spending time with some very good sapper officers and of course time with the Ghurkhas, which is never wasted.

The Ghurkhas are soldiers from Nepal, who have fought in the British Army for about 200 years. This arrangement goes back to the British conquest of India. As I understand it, when the conquering British reached the borders of Nepal, there was no strong appetite to conquer that country too and the British had been very impressed with the fighting prowess of its Ghurkha inhabitants.

A deal was struck. Nepal was not conquered, but its Ghurkha soldiers secured the right to fight in the British Army. I am roughly summarising 200 years of history here. The Ghurkhas have fought on Britain's side for two centuries and are much respected both in the British Army and beyond. Back in the nineties, there was a brigade of Ghurkhas, which if I remember rightly comprised four battalions of infantry (nearly 3000 soldiers). It was supported by a transport regiment, a signals regiment and an engineer regiment. It was the engineer regiment, the Queen's Ghurkha Engineers, that I was visiting and like the rest of the brigade, it had its base in Hong Kong. Hong Kong was still a UK colony then and no one was talking much about what would happen in 1997 when it was due to be returned to China.

Meanwhile, I thoroughly enjoyed time with these amazing soldiers and learnt a lot from their officers about what life was like in the regular 'field' army. Admittedly, Hong Kong was hardly a typical experience, but the basics remain the same. Hong Kong was certainly a change from Newcastle – it was warm for a start – but it did confirm that there was no shortage of interesting opportunities in the Royal Engineers.

On returning, I volunteered for a week or so in the Operation Raleigh offices in London, which was good experience and a good way of giving something back after the excellent time I had enjoyed in Zimbabwe the previous year.

Well, what you sow you reap, and while I was there, a vacancy occurred for a junior staff member to go and help with the expedition in Borneo that was taking place that autumn. My dilemma was that I was due to start at Sandhurst that same autumn. However, there were a considerable number of ex-army officers helping with Operation Raleigh and they all suggested I contact the Army and delay my entry by four months and start in the January intake, not September.

A simple phone call to the army and I was off to Borneo for three months, with my Sandhurst entry deferred until January. For the next three months, I had a lively time in and out of the jungle as a staff member and not a venturer as the previous year in Zimbabwe.

Borneo was a whole new experience. My role was assisting with logistics for the expedition, which often meant driving a light four-wheel-drive vehicle along impossible routes to take essential stores to one of the project sites, or bring back one of the venturers who was ill. We were in Malaysian Borneo, in the provinces of Sabah and Sarawak and it was a stunning place of contrasts. Sabah and Sarawak had all the trappings of modern civilisation in the towns and cities, with shopping malls, great roads and all the mod cons, yet sometimes barely yards away would be patches of secondary and tertiary jungle where people still lived in bamboo huts. It seemed to work, though, and Borneo came across as a happy place.

I had some close encounters which are worth recalling, especially in the jungle.

One occasion I had trekked into the jungle to visit a project site in the middle of Sarawak and bring in some medical supplies. The site was a flexible one – their task was to cut a jungle trail for walkers to see the virgin rain forest, so I knew I would have quite a stroll before I found the group along the trail they were cutting. I reached them in the early evening, and set up my 'basha', the term for a jungle shelter, in the group's camp site. A 'basha' is simply two 'A' frames from which a hammock or mattress can be suspended, with a mosquito net. The whole thing should be covered with a tarpaulin; it is the rain forest after all.

I had been rather hasty in setting up my 'basha' and I had unintentionally left a small gap between my sleeping sheet and the mosquito net. The fact that the camp site had been used for a few days meant that word had got around the local leech population, which inched its way towards the free blood-fest that had arrived. This problem is usually solved with a mosquito net and insect repellent at night, and by carefully choosing where you sit down by day.

I thought all was clear and turned in for the night. The jungle night is hardly quiet, with animal hoots and shouts, plus the odd deafening downpour of rain. But I still slept well.

However, when I awoke the next morning as camp was beginning to stir, I sensed a cigar like object rolling off my face as I sat up. More worrying, I found myself blind in one eye. I asked the nearest Operation Raleigh venturer to have a look and she immediately worked out what had happened.

During the night, a leech had wriggled into my 'basha' through the gap I had inadvertently left. It had fixed itself onto the corner of my eye socket by the bridge of my nose, and as I snored away lying on my back it had enjoyed a good night's drinking at my expense.

It had drunk so much of my blood that it was full and had detached itself from me just before dawn; that was the cigar-like object I had brushed away. However, leeches inject an anti-coagulant into the blood so that their imbibing is as easy as possible. So even when the leech had finished, my blood kept flowing. Sleeping on my back meant that my eye socket filled up with blood, which dried and hardened in time for the dawn.

It was all solved with a damp sponge and much sniggering from the Operation Raleigh people.

The second event was when I once again trekked into the rain forest to collect one of the group leaders who needed to leave the jungle for a few days. It was good practice to walk in at least pairs in the jungle, though obviously, I did a reasonable amount of solo trekking by exception.

I collected the group leader, a serving army officer who had trained with the British Army parachute regiment and therefore not lacking in fitness, and we set off back out of the jungle. We were racing the clock, because there was not enough daylight left to get out of the jungle, but we reckoned we could reach an old campsite which was an easy prospect for an overnight stay under the green canopy.

But it clouded over and rained, and rained, and rained. It became so dark that the day was shortening by at least an hour, making our race to the campsite even more aspirational. Yet I felt in my spirit we could do it, so I reckoned we should press on. He, being ex-para, agreed.

It was pouring down and we were both soaked through, that warm deluge unrelenting as we trudged along the path with the light gradually failing. The rain made so much noise it deafened our footsteps. On bursting into a jungle clearing in the gloom, we came literally face to face with a family of feeding orangutans, the 'old-men-of-the-forest', only a few feet away. I don't know who was most surprised and shocked. They screamed out deafeningly at us and raced up into the trees, while I nearly qualified for a brown trouser award.

We picked up the path and trekked on, me convinced we were nearly there and trusting the Lord, the ex-para getting less convinced. Finally, when we could barely see our hands in front of our faces, we stopped on the trail. I had to admit defeat. We were both drenched and worse, both our head torches were not working. Reluctantly, we settled down for the night, sleeping on the ground as the rain came down. There was no way either of us were going looking for sticks to make a 'basha' in the darkness with no torch; it is all too easy to get lost in the dark jungle.

It was a horrible night on the jungle floor, wrapped in a tarpaulin with the mosquito net round my face. I could feel insects and rodents investigating my reclined form; thankfully no snakes came to call. The only other benefit was that there were hardly any leeches along that deserted part of the trail; their bush telegraph was not that efficient.

The dawn came and I have seldom been so happy to see the weak rays of the early morning sun, as they peered through the sodden rain forest foliage and showed us where we were. We were 50 yards short of the campsite.

It was such a lesson to me to keep trusting in the Lord, even when my natural senses tell me otherwise. I know it is more complicated when it is not just you involved, but had I persevered a further 50 yards our night in the jungle would have been considerably more comfortable. The waiting camp had all the A frames in place and was in a clearing where we would probably have had enough light to get set up. If only I had kept us going a little longer. How often in our walk with the Lord is our life a simple matter of just keeping on keeping on going? It is so easy to stop prematurely and miss the blessing, whilst the Lord is training us to persevere to 'take hold of that for which Christ Jesus took hold of you,' as Philippians 3:12 urges us to do.

Still, the ex-para and I got on well, and went on to climb Mount Kinabalu together, Borneo's highest mountain. Highly recommended if you get the chance.

As if I had run short of evidence that the Lord protects those who know Him, I had further confirmation along the Borneo coast. Once again, I was taking medical supplies to a project site which was doing footbridge building to join up some sections of a coastal hiking route. The footbridges were to span the many small rivers that flowed through the mudflats and out to sea. No mountainous jungle here, just a wide coastal plain, littered with mangrove, sand and mud, with the odd fresh watercourse draining into the ocean.

I left the car at the last village and set off to walk along the path for the seven or so miles to where the group were. Their bridges were good and I made good progress. There was one seriously wide river on my route which was too wide for a simple footbridge, but some fishermen lived nearby who operated a simple ferry to cross the 100m wide river.

I reached the ferry crossing at midday. It was scorching hot, but alas I had the place to myself. No fishermen in sight, nor a ferry. And I had medical supplies that I needed to get to the project site. So I improvised. Tantalizingly, I could see that the path continued the other side of the slow flowing, muddy estuarine river.

I had endured an army outward bound course in Wales a few years before, and one of its lessons had been on how to use your clothes to make a flotation pack to get you and your equipment across the water. This was the time to apply some learning. I stripped off my clothes (I kept my shorts on, thank you very much, I do have *some* standards to which I adhere) and wrapping it all in the jungle tarpaulin I had with me, produced a decent flotation pack.

This floated and so into the river it went, closely followed by me. Pushing the pack in front of me, I swam steadily across the sluggish watercourse. At the halfway point, and getting my bearings as I swam, I noticed something I had not seen before. A sign, like a road sign, on the far bank, near where the path re-started. I remember musing to myself that it was unusual to see something like that in a Borneo jungle location and edged slowly closer, so I could read the lettering, wiping the water from my eyes to do so.

And the lettering was in English and it said:

"Danger. Crocodiles. Do not swim here. Please use the ferry."

Well, in an instant my genteel 'doggy paddle' across the river turned into Olympian front crawl to the far bank. I was dragging the flotation pack, not pushing it by the time my feet touched the river bed and I surged up the far bank like a D-Day landing craft, leaving a wake like a speedboat.

But I was home and, in a few minutes under that sun, dry. Clothes back on and the trek continued. On the way back the ferry men were there and were very amused when I explained how I had crossed the river. Once again, the Lord had His hand upon me.

And at the end of these three enjoyable months in Borneo, it was time to continue the career path that the Lord had for me and start my army career in earnest. I therefore had to adjust quickly from the steaming rainforests of Borneo, to the shivering winter of southern Britain.

My officer training, at the Royal Military Academy, Sandhurst, was about to begin.

Chapter 3 - Sandhurst

Psalm 25. Of David.

¹ In you, LORD my God, I put my trust.
² I trust in you; do not let me be put to shame, nor let my enemies triumph over me.
³ No one who hopes in you will ever be put to shame, but shame will come on those who are treacherous without cause.
⁴ Show me your ways, LORD, teach me your paths.
⁵ Guide me in your truth and teach me, for you are God my Saviour, and my hope is in you all day long.
⁶ Remember, LORD, your great mercy and love, for they are from of old.
⁷ Do not remember the sins of my youth and my rebellious ways; according to your love remember me, for you, LORD, are good.'

* * * * *

'Sandhurst! Sandhuuuurst…Shun!'

The Academy Sergeant Major barked the words of command and called the ranks of blue clad officer cadets to attention on the Sovereign's parade. It was a cold, grey December day with a stiff breeze cutting across the parade square. We had just listened to Princess Michael of Kent, representing the Sovereign, giving us a high level, well intentioned speech on how to be better officers and now it was time to march off.

The parade square of the Royal Military Academy, Sandhurst echoed as its officer cadets crashed to attention in unison. On the cry 'Sholdahh...Hahms! Kerwick...Mahch!' we shouldered our rifles, quick marched off the parade square and up the steps of the Old College building, thus concluding the sovereign's parade. This was mine and about two hundred fellow officer cadets' 'passing out parade', a graduation ceremony at the military academy.

It was the culmination of twelve very intensive months learning the basic art, science and craft of military leadership. All our instructors were at great pains to point out that the real lessons started when a newly commissioned officer arrived at his or her unit in the regular army. The previous year had been an unforgettable cocktail of military training, physical exertion and mental pressure. The Commissioning Course at the Royal Military Academy, Sandhurst (or simply 'Sandhurst') is a unique educational process and is viewed as a world class experience. Yet I must admit that my overwhelming experience on marching up those steps was one of profound relief that it was all over.

I have reflected on how to best describe my year at the Royal Military Academy, Sandhurst. I have chosen to relate a series of incidents and anecdotes which try to strike a balance. I wish to be faithful to my intention of making this book an encouragement for Christians and readable, so I have deliberately not produced a Sandhurst diary.

It should have been a high point of my career, an internationally renowned military college producing excellent officers... I should have loved it. But for much of it, sadly, I didn't.

As I reflect why, there are many reasons. I was certainly not in the best frame of mind for it when I started, having come straight from helping to support an Operation Raleigh expedition in Borneo. All good experience but bobbing in and out of the tropical rain forest was a poor preparation for the relentless pace of Sandhurst in winter. This meant I was 'back termed' after my first term. This was an infuriating situation because in the words of the Sandhurst Commandant who interviews all back termers, I had been 'trying too hard and needed to not push myself so much'. Back terming meant that I moved across to a different training platoon and in effect started again.

This would have been acceptable, and my training would have continued, albeit a little delayed. However, my new training platoon was not a happy one. It was referred to by others across Sandhurst as 'Penal Platoon'.

When I arrived at the new platoon my new fellow platoon members welcomed me to 'Penal Platoon' with no humour at all. They added with grim, weary irony, 'We take it in turns to be penal person'. This did not look good and unfortunately I was rapidly to become one of the 'Penal Persons'.

On joining 'Penal Platoon', so much of the rest of my time at Sandhurst seemed to be that of endeavouring to escape the wrong kind of spotlight from my new Platoon Commander. I was to learn that not everyone likes Christians, and while I am not trying to blame all my woes on one person, I believe I would have a strong case for bullying by today's standards. At the time, I only understood that I had to endure it and carry on as best I could because I was being trained for a tough profession. In other words, I chose to put up and shut up.

Yet I found for the first time in my walk with the Lord that you can have enemies, but they do not ultimately triumph over you. The Lord does not forget his sons and daughters, even if it can feel like it sometimes. This is another reason why I like

Nehemiah. He is very real about the challenges he faced from people who did not share his faith.

I will not name my Platoon Commander; I forgave him a long time ago and have no wish for any form of vengeance or retribution or compensation. I only hope that he is reconciled to God through Jesus Christ, for his own sake. Jesus tells us in Mark 6:12 to:

> *'Forgive us our debts, as we also have forgiven our debtors.'*

And so, I have moved on from that situation. I wanted the Lord to be able to forgive me my sins and my refusing to forgive others can impede the Lord forgiving me. And I don't want that to happen. Also, it leaves me free from bitterness and able to walk, not limp, on my journey with the Lord.

In the end the Lord saw me through the Valley of the Shadow, as He promises in Psalm 23, but my route through it was longer and darker than I had wanted. True to His Word, the Lord did not let me be put to shame without enabling me to triumph, in the appropriate sense, over my enemies. And by forgiving freely there is no way a Christian can be defeated.

So I will include my year at the Royal Military Academy Sandhurst in this book because it also has lessons that I believe are relevant to Christians today and because of course it was not all bad. I would add that most officers enjoyed their time there as officer cadets, but a surprisingly number had similar experiences to me.

In contrast, despite the challenges with my Platoon Commander and his manner, the Platoon Colour Sergeant was one of the best soldiers I ever met. An experienced Senior Non-Commissioned Officer (SNCO) of the Coldstream Guards, he had soldiered for many years and was very seasoned. He commanded respect by his manner and bearing. He was always professional, always ahead of the game and whilst being a very firm disciplinarian, he had a strong sense of decency. His lessons on infantry skills were superb and I kept full concentration. Most memorable were his counter-terrorism lessons. The reader must remember this was before 9/11 and the terrorists we learned about were the IRA, against whom most of us could expect to serve on operational tours during our time with the British Army. Our Colour Sergeant had completed many such tours as an infantryman and was replete with relevant experience which he shared in a professional, non-gratuitous way. We respected him deeply and he enshrined those characteristics of courage, loyalty, professionalism, aggression, humour and determination which to me makes the exemplar soldier. The extent to which these attributes must apply to an exemplar Christian would be a good discussion topic.

In effect, he carried the platoon and towards the end of my time at Sandhurst I even saw the mask slip a little as the frustration of his having to 'manage-up' the Platoon Commander began to show.

I still believe Sandhurst to be an excellent institution, and recognise that had different personalities been involved, my experience would have been very different.

So, what is the Royal Military Academy, Sandhurst?

It is a vast military training facility just outside London and has been where the British Army has trained the majority of its regular army officers for the past hundred or more years. It has accommodation blocks, sports pitches, assault courses, rifle ranges, gymnasia, swimming facilities, classrooms, lecture theatres, stables, logistics areas and outdoor training areas. It is the UK equivalent of the USA's West Point.

It is divided into three colleges: Old College, New College and Victory College. The most recognised image of Sandhurst is of course Old College, where at the end of the Sovereign's Passing Out Parade the officer cadets who have been commissioned that day are allowed the privilege of marching up its steps and into the building. The unusual tradition is that they are followed by the parade adjutant on his horse who also go up the steps and into Old College; I remember moving out of the beast's (the horse, not the adjutant) way as it came through the door immediately behind the rest of us.

To a newcomer in the early 90s, Sandhurst was quite an intimidating place. Funnily enough, I saw a documentary on the current Sandhurst training of officer cadets quite recently and was struck by how little had changed.

It is still the officer training school for the British Army, and officer recruits are called officer cadets. They are grouped into training platoons of about 30 cadets each. Each platoon is led by the Platoon Commander who is a senior captain, usually a high-flying officer from the regular army. Sandhurst trains its officer cadets in the basics of infantry command and so its platoon captains are mainly from British Army infantry regiments. My memorable platoon commander came from one of those infantry regiments. However, in the interests of fairness and because every person in the army is trained to be a soldier first, suitable captains from other parts of the army such as the Royal Artillery, the Royal Engineers and tank regiments (still referred to as cavalry regiments in the British Army!) also serve as Platoon Commanders at Sandhurst.

Assisting the Platoon Commander is a Colour Sergeant. Traditionally, they are often from one of the Foot Guards Regiments (most familiarly seen 'Trooping the Colour' each year) or from another infantry regiment. There are also Staff Sergeants from the rest of the army. I say assisting the Platoon

Commander, because it does appear that the Colour Sergeant does the bulk of the work; certainly, in the first half of the officer training year.

These Colour Sergeants are the characters that officer cadets at Sandhurst remember the most. It is an unusual working relationship that goes back nearly 100 years, whereby the traditionally working class Colour Sergeants of Sandhurst have the authority to shape, mould and form the traditionally 'upper' class officer cadets who will be the officers of the future British Army. The irony is that the Colour Sergeants must call the officer cadets 'Sir' and then they can be as rude as they like with them, providing no bullying takes place; the methodology is about always wanting to produce a good officer at the end of it.

Generally, it works extremely well and it thrives on mutual respect. The Colour Sergeants are all aware of how important it is to train up the next generation of army officers. Getting it wrong and producing officers not up to the job will not help the army or their fellow soldiers.

There are so many funny stories illustrating this relationship, some of them repeatable in a Christian book. I heard one exasperated Colour Sergeant scream at an officer cadet:

'If brains was chocolate, yours would not fill a smartie, Sir!'.

Or on parade, a surprised large Colour Sergeant to a very petite female officer cadet:

'You are no bigger than a fridge magnet, Ma'am!'

This can be even more amusing for the Sergeant Majors, who are always called 'Sir' by non-officers and who must call officers 'Sir'. There was an occasion where an impertinent new officer cadet asked one of the Sergeant Majors why he the officer cadet had to call the Sergeant major 'Sir'? And yet the Sergeant Major also had to call him, the officer cadet, 'Sir'.

There was a thunderous silence while those within earshot blenched in anticipation of a deafening tirade. It never came. Instead, the Sergeant Major responded with an indignant yet restrained growl, 'Well Sir, the difference is this. *You* mean it.'

On still another occasion, a Colour Sergeant was briefing his platoon on the location of their next training exercise. It was Pippingford Park, in Kent, immediately adjacent to where AA Milne wrote his famous children's stories featuring Christopher Robin, et al. The cockney Colour Sergeant addressed his platoon:

'Sirs, we is off to Pippingford Park on a training exercise. Do any of you educmacayted gennelmen know what Pippingford Park is famous for?'

A puzzled silence was the platoon's only reply.

'Whaaat?' roared the Colour Sergeant, 'Avent none of you gennelmen ever read *any* books?'

Still no word of recognition from the platoon.

'Sirs', snarled the now disgusted Colour Sergeant 'It's where Winnie the Pooh cuts abaht!' Cutting about is a southern English idiom for moving briskly…

Therefore, the Sandhurst training regime is underpinned by the understanding that the Colour Sergeants and Sergeant Majors have the experience and expertise needed to develop the latent qualities within officer cadets in order for them to become good officers. This formality is preserved for the serious business of training tomorrow's army officers to be its future junior commanders, and in turn its future majors, colonels and generals.

The Sandhurst Common Commissioning Course starts with basic soldier training which includes a lot of drill or 'square bashing' where officer cadets are taught to march. This is a surprisingly good way of building teamwork and interdependence. We also spent a lot of time polishing and cleaning and generally maintaining the military kit with which we were issued. We worked long hours to keep the kit immaculate; whole weeks of four hours sleep per night was not uncommon because of daily room inspections ('Stand by your beds!'), kit inspections, preparing for the next day's lesson or cleaning kit after the previous day's exertions. The slightest mistake or blemish and it all had to be done again. It was a way of preparing you to overcome disappointment and setbacks but could be very demoralising when you had been sweating for hours the night before, trying to get it right first time!

We grew wise to some ways of saving effort. Once our folded bed blocks had met with the colour sergeant's approval, most of us slept in our sleeping bags on the floor of our rooms to avoid the hassle of refolding them ever again. This is all done at a rapid pace, with rushed meals and seemingly 48 hours of work crammed into 24. In this phase, the Colour Sergeant is seemingly omnipotent and is always on your back, wanting things done quicker, better and demanding a reason if not. We were regularly reminded that if you look after your kit, then your kit will look after you. The British Army insists on very high standards of personal turn out and maintenance of equipment.

Sandhurst Colour Sergeants are always immaculately turned out and seemingly each one has at least fifteen uniforms ready to go, complete with gleaming boots at their immediate disposal; I never saw a scruffy Colour Sergeant. They appear like genies when you least expect them, checking that you are preparing your kit, or polishing your shoes, or learning infantry formations, or the different ranks of the Army, or the rate of fire of infantry weapons. One tall, gaunt Grenadier Guards Colour Sergeant earned the generally affectionate nickname 'The Screaming Skull' for his regular manifestations from nowhere, demanding more perfection of his platoon.

A small minority of Colour Sergeants just shouted at their platoons all the time, without leavening this with their experience and harnessing their officer cadets' desire to learn. They squandered the respect of their platoons because of their narrow approach.

However, most Colour Sergeants balanced their terrifying persona with the wisdom that comes with handling soldiers and people. In the majority of cases, they were greatly respected and admired by their platoons of officer cadets.

As the course progressed, so the focus shifted from basic training to officer training, where the officer cadets are given opportunities to lead during exercises in the field. A key theme of the training regime at Sandhurst is to teach an officer cadet how to be a soldier and a leader at the same time by putting them in command positions so that they have to lead, even when they don't feel like it. This was not always what you wanted when tired out after two days into a five-day full on infantry training exercise in the Brecon Beacon Mountains in Wales, but you had no choice in the matter and that was the point. Sandhurst was fundamentally about training leaders. And leaders must lead whether they feel like it or not.

These 'command appointments' as they were called, came thick and fast and meant that an officer cadet became in charge of that part of the platoon or section (part of the platoon) for that phase of the exercise. Many people did not enjoy them because you were in the spotlight and shouted at more than usual. It was a brutal yet accurate way of establishing whether an officer cadet had learned the necessary lessons that he or she would need when they eventually became a commissioned officer. And when it went wrong, everybody knew!

Handled well, this sink or swim approach works well because it tests whether leadership is being developed or not. Handled badly, it then becomes an opportunity for people to be humiliated and I do not believe that anyone learns well when being humiliated. While people make mistakes and these mistakes can be funny, there is a fine line between laughing *with* someone and laughing *at* someone. My Platoon Commander's sarcastic approach to training his platoon did not inspire most of the platoon members and was humiliating. My main lesson from this was to make sure that, assuming I made it to becoming a commissioned officer, I would not treat my future soldiers like that.

I had to be careful of my attitude though. My Platoon Commander was still my Platoon Commander. It is an easy thing to challenge and criticise those in leadership and authority, but very different when it is you doing the leading. This is an inconvenient truth today, where leadership and authority are routinely challenged, especially in the culture of the western hemisphere. As I read the Scriptures, especially the New Testament, so much of Christianity is about leading; be it any form of ministry or simply living out the Christian life. Leading is what a Christian is, as well as does. Whether we are in class, at home, in an office, part of a team or its CEO, Christians are expected to lead or at least influence those around them. And we are expected to respect and honour those in authority, too.

The motto of the Royal Military Academy Sandhurst is 'Serve to Lead' which is a surprise when you consider the popular autocratic and 'top down' stereotype of military leadership. A few years after I was commissioned and having compared Sandhurst experiences with fellow officers, I was reassured to find how much 'Serve to Lead' had been practised by their Platoon Commanders at Sandhurst. The common theme was the humble gentlemanliness of the average Sandhurst Platoon Commander, whilst in no way compromising the firm, determined style of command that is a hallmark of the British Army officer.

This has stood me in excellent stead in life because if you look the part without shouting your mouth off, it goes a long way towards establishing credibility. This is a valuable life lesson. I have visited a shop in scruffy jeans and tee shirt and days later received a totally different reception when wearing collar and tie in the same shop. People do respond well when you look the part, despite how clueless you may feel inside! While it is always important to know what you are talking about, looking the part is more important than you might think.

Of course, the ultimate servant leader was, and is, Jesus Christ though I am not sure to what extent that view resonates across the Royal Military Academy at Sandhurst! Reading the gospels shows how Jesus never stopped leading and He repeatedly 'spoke as one who had authority'. Yet without being servile Himself, He never stopped serving those around Him.

So, back to penal platoon. My fellow officer cadets were a good bunch in the main. As the influence of our Platoon Commander increased, as the officer training aspect of the course developed, so my time at Sandhurst grew less pleasant. I felt that there was nothing I could do right in this man's eyes and his sarcastic, humiliating approach was starting to wear me down. The other officer cadets began to comment and quietly ask me what I had done to irritate him. I really did not know. I have said before that I was not a perfect recruit, but I was not abysmal either and I had seen enough of the regular army to know that the Sandhurst routine and training experience is in no way typical of the field army. Yes, Sandhurst is an accepted rite of passage, but thankfully the Sandhurst culture is not representative of another day in the Corps of Royal Engineers, to which I was headed.

A man can get very demoralised when life feels like this and I cannot stress enough how important it is for a Christian to have fellowship, so one of the key lessons through this for me was the utter necessity of securing intelligent fellowship in my workplace. As I look back over my Christian life thus far, whenever I have struggled to 'walk the walk', the absence of good fellowship has been a factor. Ultimately, we all must walk out our own paths with the Lord, but fellowship that strengthens and encourages (and allows you to do the same for others) is a critical component of a Christian's life. We are designed to be part of a body, a family, an army(!) and lone rangers are not normally part of God's plan. The Lord said of Adam in Genesis 2:18 'It is not good for the man to be alone' and that has even bigger implications than just marriage. For any Christian, finding decent 'intelligent' fellowship is critical because there is always someone else to help, and none of us are that good that we do not need help from someone else. Wars are not won by individual actions.

I say 'intelligent'. What I mean is fellowship that has a level of understanding for the trials you are facing. I found it hard to describe the difficulties I was having to my Christian pals from Newcastle University, because I might has well have been on another planet. My life was now so different to theirs. Intensive route marches across army training areas, being roared at, and assimilating a new military lifestyle are very different to the experiences of a final year of university or new recruit to most other jobs. I just did not know what to tell people, especially my Christian friends, about Sandhurst.

Thankfully the Lord had already thought of that and a longstanding organisation called the Officers' Christian Union (OCU) was on hand. The OCU had been around since Victorian times as a prayer union for British military officers. Since 2005, it has quite rightly welcomed all ranks from all three Services in its fellowship and changed its name to the Armed Forces' Christian Union (AFCU). It was then, and remains now, an excellent source of prayer support, fellowship and wisdom for those called to serve Jesus in the UK Armed Forces.

One of its leading lights back then was a Christian couple who were known to dozens of young officers and officer cadets like me. He had been an officer for twenty years and, when he left the Army, they both felt that God wanted them to minister to young officers and officer cadets. Therefore, they bought a house a few miles from Sandhurst and he also served as the General Secretary of the OCU. To me they were the provision of the Lord, because they encouraged me and challenged me in my walk with God. They never offered me the soft option, but they loved the Lord deeply, had a wonderful gift of hospitality and their military background meant that they understood something of the trials I was facing. They offered a military Christian benchmark upon which to gauge what was going on.

Meanwhile my public berating at the hands of my Platoon Commander for my inability to shape up to his expectation of a future officer continued. Matters finally came to a head following a defining episode that occurred during a training run in full kit through some woodland.

The Army does like to make its training realistic and therefore it is quite common for it to spring surprises to replicate the unplanned nature of warfare. So, as we were running past a conveniently positioned wide plank of wood in the forest, the Platoon Commander called out to one of the platoon officer cadets: 'You are now the casualty; the rest of you, carry him and his kit'.

The officer cadet was placed carefully on the plank of wood, which was carried in relays by most of the platoon and his equipment distributed amongst the rest. He was a cheerful chap and as we bowled along, he caught my attention and said:

'Cor, Mark, I bet I remind you of Jesus, stretched out on a plank of wood like this; though at least I am not nailed to it!'

I smiled because he was teasing me, not offending me and I made a suitable remark back about his needing to watch out for unexpected lightning strikes if he made comments like that. The run continued and I thought no more about it, but the Platoon Commander had overheard the exchange...

With no warning the next morning I was marched in to see him in his office. There, as I stood to attention in front of his desk, he informed me that he had observed the conversation on the plank of wood and what did I think about it?

I did not understand the problem, so I asked what the difficulty was? My Platoon Commander was sitting in his chair and leant forward towards me. In his opinion, he declared frankly, my future soldiers would think I was weird for having Christian beliefs; so I needed to think about my future in the army very seriously.

All I could do was reply that I could still not see why it was a problem. He dismissed me with a back handed wave; it was not my best interview experience. Later, on a platoon training exercise, the Platoon Commander decided that the platoon would run back to camp as a squad; except me. I was to make my own way back because he did not deem me fit to be in his unit.

So, I made my solo journey back to the accommodation in Sandhurst. I must admit I reached my lowest point then and as I plodded back, I faced heaven and asked the Lord to take this British Army 'chalice' away from me. I had had enough. I had no idea it would be so unpleasant and I had no desire to continue with this demeaning and degrading training process. I wanted out. I would find another job, another career.

And then the Lord spoke to me. He said that it was His plan, not mine, that I was in the Army and that He would see me through, and that I did not have the right to quit.

As you can imagine, this was not the answer I wanted, but was the answer I received, so I asked for help to continue…and so I continued…and I did not quit.

Clearly administrative military wheels were turning behind the scenes because a few days later I was summoned to the office of the Officer Commanding (OC). The OC was a major, commanding the three platoons of the Training Company of which my 'Penal Platoon' was one; he was my Platoon Commander's boss. It was no surprise to learn that my Platoon Commander really did not like me and really did want me out of the army. It transpired that my Christian faith had been mentioned as a factor more than once. My Platoon Commander had been having some conversations with the OC about this and the OC wanted to see me for himself. Hence why I was standing at attention in front of his desk; another Sandhurst interview.

As the OC talked, I perceived that he was not enamoured with my Platoon Commander. While the OC was too professional to say so, the way he leant back in his chair, put his hands together and made a steeple out of his fingers told me he was choosing his words carefully. The Company Sergeant Major was in attendance, if nothing else to march me in and out, but he too must have had some input.

The OC tactfully pointed out that I still had much to learn as a potential officer in the British Army, but unlike my Platoon Commander he failed to see why being a Christian would prevent me from being a good officer. In fact, commented the OC, he had observed me to maintain my Christian values and principles amid considerable challenge, which was more than he could say for the way that many of my colleagues stuck to their values. Therefore, he was overruling the wishes of my Platoon Commander.

I was in. And thus, the Lord's plan was carried out as He had told me a few days before at my low point. Thereafter the storm from my Platoon Commander abated and I was, relatively speaking, left alone to continue my training as a member of the platoon; now there was no chance of the Platoon Commander ejecting me, I was no longer routinely singled out. Which did wonders for my motivation and I found myself learning better as a result.

Amidst the rapid pace of lessons, drill on the square and exercises ranging from night navigation, to urban warfare, to anti-terrorism operations, Sandhurst had its lighter moments. I need to recount some of these if nothing else to get the balance right.

On exercise in the Welsh mountains, the platoon was tasked to ambush a group of 'enemy' along a forestry road by night. Now Sandhurst uses a company of Ghurkha soldiers as enemy for all its exercises, and they were great characters. Ghurkhas are superb soldiers and possess a great sense of humour. When 'shot' on exercise they would 'die' with the most dramatic howls, cries and spasms of pain. They would qualify for an Oscar with their passionate amateur dramatics and it certainly lightened the moment. Ghurkhas still use the word 'Sahib' when talking to an officer instead of the English word 'Sir', which is an interesting relic from previous generations of British Army soldiering in days of empire. It goes without saying that Ghurkha infantry skills are top notch. They would be a quality 'enemy' and we knew our ambush would have to be good.

To make it realistic, we all were expecting to lie in wait for up to 12 hours before we could spring the ambush. In real terms for our training exercise, at some point during those 12 hours through the night the Ghurkha enemy platoon would stroll down the road to be summarily mown down by our blank firing weapons. And 'die' dramatically. This still required excellent communication and vigilance for the 12-hour period by the platoon, because the timing of the order to 'open fire' and the ensuing firefight still needed to be well conducted so that no enemy could claim they could escape. Ambushes must be well planned and everyone needs to be clear of their location, role and responsibilities in laying an ambush. Timing is key. Ambushes are not as simple as they appear in the films.

However, this was three days into a four-day exercise and most of us had slept very little during that time. Our normally ever-present Colour Sergeant had been called away and our Platoon Commander was not around. So none of the 'grown-ups', as we called them, were supervising us. As we took up our fire positions (lying on soft pine needles, with rifles pointing at where the enemy was expected) on a warm dry night, it was clear that the biggest challenge would be to stay awake.

An early indication of this problem was when a friend of mine in his fire position beside me, not only fell asleep, but had a nightmare and then woke himself up by calling out loudly and incoherently into the darkness. Thankfully, no enemy were near. From the mutters and grunts across the platoon position in the darkness, he was obviously not the only one who had been woken up. Peace returned and the vigil continued.

What must have been a few hours later, I felt a firm hand shaking my shoulder and a strange voice saying, 'Wake up, Sahib!'. It was one of the Ghurkhas! How had they got into our platoon ambush position?

What had happened was that the Ghurkhas had been quietly walking down the forestry track without making a sound, waiting to be ambushed by us. They had heard the sounds of the entire platoon fast asleep and snoring loudly. Guessing what had happened, and not wishing to get us in trouble with our notorious Platoon Commander, they had crept into our position and woken us all up. They then nipped back up the forestry track and again strolled down the forestry track as planned. The platoon, now being wide awake, conducted a faultless ambush and everyone was happy…and not a word was breathed to the Platoon Commander about the actual circumstances.

On what I hope is more of a historical note, as our commissioning course concluded, so we officer cadets earned the right to purchase military kit for exercise. I say a historical note, because I sincerely trust that the British Army is kitting out its soldiers and officers better than it did 'in my day!'.

We all bought tropical pattern combat trousers and shirts, which were the same pattern as our normal combat uniform but dried out quickly. As our Colour Sergeant drily remarked, our issue combat kit in those days 'Needed a thermonuclear detonation to dry properly'. Once it got wet on exercise, it stayed wet, which was not a lot of fun when you are wearing it for four to five days in winter.

We bought a wide range of kit, ranging from better drinking cups to green gaiters to keep the water out. Many of us bought better boots, sleeping bags and waterproofs. Most of us spent a three-figure sum even in those days, when you could still buy a pint of beer for under £1.

Still, this surprising retail therapy boosted our morale in anticipation of a tough two-week final exercise.

The final training exercise for our course exercise took place in France, somewhere near Limoges, (or 'Leemowhg' as the Company Sergeant Major pronounced it, thinking it rhymed with Kylie's surname). In comparison to the relentless pace we were expecting, it was a surprisingly sedate affair. Something was going on, which we never found out, but it meant that we were left by ourselves with no 'grown-ups' to make life difficult, to defend a small patch of forest in the middle of idyllic French nowhere, for about three days.

One must make do and, being the only willing French speaker in the platoon, I engaged a passing French farmer in conversation, in the interests of the Entente-Cordiale. I soon found that local farmers were very happy to drop off some vin rouge and baguettes for a few Francs for the hungry/thirsty Anglais soldat officeurs. So it was an outrageously relaxed exercise and very enjoyable; not the remorseless marching, firing, screaming inferno that most of us were expecting.

There were a few weeks remaining of the course following the final exercise, but as the Colour Sergeant put it, 'It's all over bar the shouting'. My recollection of this time is the build-up to being commissioned and knowing that the real training and learning takes place when a junior officer leaves Sandhurst and joins their regular army unit.

During this time though, I did make a serious mistake and that was to date a non-Christian girl. I make no excuses. It stemmed from my refusal to plunge into the pagan revelry that can characterise the social life organisations like the army. Many of my army friends enjoyed this kind of lifestyle, though I knew it was not to be a part of my life and so I walked accordingly. My avoidance of this lifestyle had been noted by many in my training company as well as my platoon. However, a rumour was circulated by certain of my colleagues that I was not interested in girls, with lurid implications about my sexual orientation. This was quite a shock to me. And I when I found out, I was determined to do something about it, and fast. Sadly, I did not consult the Holy Spirit.

So, at the next party that was on I met a pleasant, attractive enough girl, who was clearly not a Christian, and started to date her. Well, it scotched the rumour about my sexual orientation, but it was not a wise move on my part. Interestingly, many of my Christian friends were very supportive, citing the old line that 'surely you can lead her to the Lord!'. Hmm. I have heard that one many times since then as a comment on that kind of situation. However, on telling one of my more discerning Christian friends from university that I was no longer single, he took the trouble to write to me immediately and he quoted two scriptures:

- 1 Corinthians 6: Do you not know that your bodies are temples of the Holy Spirit, who is in you, whom you have received from God? *You are not your own; you were bought at a price.* Therefore, honour God with your body *(my italics).*
- 2 Corinthians 6:14: Do not be yoked together with unbelievers. For what do righteousness and wickedness have in common? Or what fellowship can light have with darkness?

I was immediately convicted and grudgingly grateful for a friend who had the moral courage to challenge me and prevent me from following a very wrong choice. It is such a bad idea for a Christian to go out with a non-Christian and it so often ends in tears. Do not do it. The Lord has the 'right one' for each of us that so desires and it is worth the wait. Trying to achieve in the flesh what the Lord intends in the Spirit is always a big mistake – ask Abraham!

As you know in Genesis 16, Abraham tried to start his promised family prematurely, and it caused him and his family a few difficulties thereafter.

In the end, after just two weeks I broke off the relationship at around the time I was commissioned. She was incredibly understanding and more gracious than I was. I had learned a hard lesson, which I have not repeated.

The final event was the Sovereign's Parade, with which I started this chapter. This is a big event and we rehearsed it for weeks beforehand. I understand it follows a similar format to the 'Trooping the Colour' of the Queen's birthday parade. Of course, that just meant a lot of time in our uniforms, wearing our hobnail boots and carrying rifles and practising our drill again and again and again. Then learning to do it with a band playing, which can make you lose step if the acoustics are poor. The Sergeant Majors and Colour Sergeant had a field day of course, with most of them being guardsmen and therefore knowing the parade off by heart.

On one rehearsal, one officer cadet, let's call him Mr Pacer, was responsible as 'right marker' for bringing a group of marching officer cadets to halt at the right place on the parade square in front of Old College. Failure to do this properly would put the whole parade out of position in time for the speech.

Well, this officer cadet stopped about ten paces short, which, as anticipated, put the whole parade out of position. Mr Pacer was therefore the recipient of some snarling attention from one of the Sergeant Majors, flanked by two glowering Colour Sergeants who mirrored and growled their assent to the Sergeant Major's disgusted remarks about Mr Pacer's sense of timing and direction. Mr Pacer, however, felt this was unfair and that he was in the correct position. And said so.

If the Sergeant Major was surprised at this limited defiance, he did not show it. His face hardened as he glared at Mr Pacer. The Colour Sergeants looked at each other and winced. The parade held its collective breath.

'Mr Pacer, Sir' roared the Sergeant Major, his face inches from that of Mr Pacer, and indicating with his pace-stick a small mark on the parade square ten paces away 'There is the place you should have halted. Not here. I hardly think the earth's core has shifted by ten paces since our last parade. So about turn, all of you, and we will do it all again. Courtesy of Mr Pacer'.

So back we all went and did it again, but despite the Sergeant Major's intentions, Mr Pacer's street cred had risen several notches as a consequence.

I do not know if this is still the case, but on the days prior to the Sovereign's Parade, the stable containing the Sandhurst Adjutant's white horse is guarded around the clock. This is because a few years before our parade, some enterprising officer cadets had fed it with laxative chocolate late in the evening before the parade. I will leave you to imagine the dire (or diarrhoea) results on the parade the next day, but expressions like 'Through the eye of a needle at twenty paces' were used.

Horse dung can pose a problem, and so the Academy Sergeant Major, who runs the parade, hit upon the idea of instructing the Corporal who managed the stables to be on hand with a brush and large dust pan to remove any brown offerings produced by the Adjutant's white horse.

So, for rehearsals involving the Adjutant on his horse, the Corporal was there and efficiently removed evidence of a horseman riding by. Unfortunately, the sight of the Corporal in full parade uniform marching out complete with brush and pan every time the horse had a bowel movement was just too funny for words. It was like something from 'Monty Python' and the whole parade would snigger, only to be bellowed into silence by the nearest Sergeant Major.

The Corporal was ribbed by the officer cadets about this off parade, too, to the extent that he requested an interview with the Academy Sergeant Major about it, where he respectfully pointed out that while he accepted that sometimes life in the Army can be a load of muck, he had not joined the Army to publicly shovel it. Nor had he joined the Army to be the laughing stock of over 200 future officers and would the Academy Sergeant Major, Sir, respectfully see it from his point of view?

Well, the Academy Sergeant Major listened, and in fairness to him he took the Corporal's point. The Corporal was relieved of that part of his duties which had vexed him so much. This meant of course that now steaming brown mountains could appear on the parade ground with little warning, so us officer cadets could not change pace or direction and simply had to march through and over any such obstacle in our path.

By the day of the Sovereign's Parade, us officer cadets now knew the parade very well, even if not as by heart as the Sergeant Majors and Colour Sergeants. As is the British Army way with most operations, training hard means that the actual operation or task goes much more smoothly. Which is true in life, though so often we do not make time to train and rehearse.

The parade day was cold, grey and December, but it did not matter one jot. All of us were glad to be 'passing out', and many of us were just relieved. Many of my pals had been celebrating all week with repeat trips to local pubs, which meant on the day of the Sovereign's Parade, one or two of them were somewhat hung over and looking rather green.

One of my fellow platoon members, thankfully in the rear rank, was definitely the worst for wear that morning and we were impressed that he made it to the Duchess' speech. However, that good lady's speech was not the most concise of orations and this officer cadet was starting to sway like a ship's mast. Our ever-watchful Platoon Colour Sergeant, quietly and without fuss, marched up behind up and grabbed his belt. And for the duration of the speech, the Colour Sergeant held this officer cadet upright to prevent him from keeling over and disgracing himself. The Army can be very kind like that.

It seemed moments later that the Sovereign's Parade was concluded and us Sandhurst 'graduates' were marching up the steps of Old College, closely pursued by the adjutant on his white horse. We were free to get on with the rest of our military career, in whichever part of the army we were to serve to lead.

Young, free and single, and now a commissioned officer, the next stage in my training was the Troop Commanders' Course, where young officers posted to the Royal Engineers learnt the specifics of what it was to be a Royal Engineer officer. However, there was a four-month gap until then and so several us went to different regular engineer regiments on attachment. The idea was that us newly commissioned 'sprog' officers could spend a useful few months shadowing experienced officers and learn some of the ropes of command, without doing too much damage.

I was posted to a UK based engineer regiment on Salisbury Plain in southern England, and the next stage of my military education was about to begin.

It had not been the year I was expecting. Sandhurst had taught me something of leadership, both how to do it and how *not* to do it. Clearly my experience with my Platoon Commander was not common and had made my time there far tougher than expected. The sarcastic style which he had led his platoon has been a factor in why I am such a big believer in en*courage*ment today; discouragement can rob you of key attributes like *courage*, plus others like confidence, initiative and enjoying the life that the Lord has for you. Discouragement can lead to disappointment, cynicism and bitterness. It stops you from attempting the seemingly impossible; it makes it hard for you to inspire those you lead.

Encouragement, on the other hand, is more than just saying 'well done'. It is the impartation of courage. And as Winston Churchill replied when asked 'What is the greatest virtue?', he responded 'Courage, because with courage, all other virtues are possible'.

He was absolutely right. I believe courage and encouragement have the same root word, *cour*, which means *of the heart*. If our hearts are right, everything else will follow. Which is why Jesus says in John 14:1:

> '*Do not let your hearts be troubled.*'

Encouragement, and the impartation of courage is a key component of leadership. So I did learn *something* at Sandhurst!

I have no intention of exposing the Platoon Commander's identity. If he has made his peace with the Lord, then we are brothers in Christ and will have an eternity to laugh about those months in Sandhurst. If not, then I hope and pray he does make his peace with the Lord, as must everyone who does not already know Him.

As I have mentioned before, forgiving freely liberates the Christian from bitterness and shame and though I accept that it is sometimes a difficult path for a Christian to follow, it is none the less the path Jesus expects us to walk and He is with us every step of the way.

Sandhurst was absolutely not representative of the rest of the British Army, as I was soon to find out, but its ethos is a sound one when correctly applied. 'Serve to Lead' is a fine expression of how to be in charge. I wonder how often we see it role modelled today? For a simple demonstration, I turn to a gospel or four to see how Jesus did it.

If nothing else Sandhurst was a toughening period for me and I can only say what a huge relief it was to go on attachment to the field army immediately afterwards to reacquaint myself with the soldiers and officers of the Royal Engineers. Their anticipated professionalism and manner were high on my original list of reasons for joining the British Army in the first place; they certainly did not disappoint.

Chapter 4 - The Engineer Regiment

James 1:19:

'My dear brothers, take note of this: Everyone should be quick to listen, slow to speak and slow to become angry.'

I arrived at my new regiment on Salisbury Plain and knew that military life was now different for me. In many respects, my military education was only just beginning.

I was now an officer, though on the lowest rung of the ladder as a mere Second Lieutenant (pronounced Lefttenant in the British Army, a Loo-tenant is someone living in a water closet). My badge of rank was a simple 'pip' worn on each shoulder, denoting my 'officer' status.

Towards the end of the commissioning course at Sandhurst, our wise Colour Sergeant had talked about what it was to be an officer and he said that he saluted the rank and not the person. I think in part this helped him to deal with the Platoon Commander, but there was humbling wisdom in what he said. Otherwise, being saluted risks going to a person's head. Of course, when an officer is saluted, he or she must return the salute.

I found that grinning soldiers of the Royal Engineers liked to time their salutes to perfection. This normally meant saluting an officer like me at just the point when I was just getting off my bike and needed both hands. Saluting in a dignified manner whilst dismounting a bike takes a little practice if you and it are not to end up in a tangled heap, to the accompaniment of a chorus of 'Do you need any help, Sir?!' Or they would salute with the left hand to see if I would notice. Or the more awkward soldiers would simply not salute and see what happened.

This was a good test and it only happened to me once. I pulled up the soldier in question, explained that he could think what he liked about me personally, but that he had to salute my rank. He saluted. Problem solved, but woe betide an officer who did not pull up a soldier who failed to salute them; the officer would risk being despised.

I was now a commissioned officer in the Royal Engineers, but what are the Royal Engineers and what do they do? When I asked that question I received the very simple answer: The Royal Engineers exist to enable the rest of the army to live, move and fight, and to prevent the enemy from doing the same.

In the nineties, the roles of the Royal Engineers in wartime were summarised:

- Mobility (e.g. Bridge building, mine clearance, route repair, etc.)
- Counter-mobility (e.g. Bridge demolition, mine laying and laying obstacles, etc.)
- Helping the Army to live, move and fight (e.g. Building camps, supplying water, etc.)

The Royal Engineers (or the Corps of Royal Engineers) has been around for over three hundred years and has been in support of the British Army throughout that time. Any Royal Engineer is known as a 'Sapper', which comes from a zig zag sap trench dug by an attacker toward an enemy line of defence, so that the enemy cannot fire directly into the trench as it approaches his line of defence. 'Sapper' is also the designation of a private soldier in the Royal Engineers, just as it is 'Gunner' in the Royal Artillery, or 'Signaller' in the Royal Signals, for example.

It was Royal Engineers who helped build the railways in Canada and India; a Royal Engineer even built the Albert Hall in London (not by himself!). It was the Royal Engineers who supervised the construction of the trenches in the First World War. From the Royal Engineers came the Royal Signals, the Royal Electrical and Mechanical Engineers and even (it can be argued, though they won't admit it!) the Royal Air Force.

Please do not assume that the Royal Engineers are confined to support. One of the mottos of the Royal Engineers is 'Ubique', which is Latin for 'Everywhere', because that is where Royal Engineers must be on the battlefield. And this can be right up on the front line. The sappers who cleared the mines for the Army to advance at the battle of El Alamein were at the point of the Allied advance. As were the armoured engineers in their specially designed obstacle clearance tanks on D-Day. Bridge building is the other Royal Engineer task at which sappers excel and whenever the army advances, there are usually a horde of sweating sappers ensuring the bridges are in place so that it doesn't get its tanks wet. There is a glossary at the end of this book which gives a fuller explanation of the British Army in general and the Royal Engineers in more detail.

Their role is crucial to the success of the British Army. Indeed, Field Marshall Montgomery was famously quoted as saying that there were 'never enough sappers' during the Second World War. And he knew a thing or two about leading successful armies.

What was it like being in the regular army?

It was a breath of fresh air after Sandhurst and a whole new learning experience. While as an officer I had rank, I was very much the new boy and knew I had a lot to learn from the experienced soldiers and officers at the Engineer Regiment.

I was told early on that a new officer had two ears and one mouth, as the quote from the Book of James at the beginning of this chapter implies. Therefore, the idea was to listen and learn rather than strive to impress everyone on day one. It is a difficult balance. On one hand, you know that you are an officer and your job is to lead; you outrank all the soldiers from the RSM down and technically they must do what you say. On the other hand, they have experience and wisdom on which to draw and so the knack is tapping into that wisdom, without losing sight of the fact that if the crunch comes, the officer makes the decision.

This is why opportunities to spend a few weeks or months on attachment are such a good idea, because for a brief period a new officer has a chance to ask questions without being saddled with massive responsibility. I realise that not everyone has this luxury; plenty of newly commissioned officers take over troops or platoons on day one, even on operations, and learn on the job from there.

My attachment was with what was known as the AMF(L) Troop, a large sapper field troop which was set aside to be on standby to deploy anywhere in Europe on behalf of Allied Command Europe (ACE). Something of a left over from the cold war, the ACE Mobile Land Force or AMF(L) was a multinational force that could be rapidly deployed to any part of the ACE area of operations from eastern Turkey to northern Norway and all of Europe in between. Its purpose was to show the resolve of the NATO alliance and its ability to resist all forms of aggression against any member state.

I was expecting to go on exercise to northern Norway, as the AMF(L) Troop normally did at that time of year, but just then matters were deteriorating in Yugoslavia, soon to fragment into its constituent parts and become the Former Republic of Yugoslavia. So, the AMF(L) Troop was put on standby for that part of the world, all the vehicles were painted in the United Nation livery of dull white with the initials 'UN' on the side. And we stayed in Salisbury Plain, which was a slight disappointment.

However, in Christ nothing is ever wasted and it meant I could spend time learning the ropes.

The officers at the Engineer Regiment were a great bunch and very sociable. Every Thursday night was a 'Curry Club' where the living in members of the Officer Mess would pile into a few cars and visit a different Indian restaurant. Spending time with these guys, many of whom had deployed on the First Gulf War a few years before, was a valuable experience. On reflection, I think I learned that it is very important as a leader to not compromise who you are.

I learned though, especially in a military environment where you are very visible as an officer, that being a Christian is like living in a goldfish bowl. Your every action is observed and noted. I used to play a lot of squash and after work a group of us officers would use the regimental squash courts for a few matches. I thought I was quite good, but some of my colleagues could stand in the middle of the court and swat the ball as one would a slow wasp, while I would spend the entire match racing up and down the court after the next expertly placed lob, trying to stop my shot from going back to the centre. Whereupon the other player would gently swipe the ball into another corner…and I would chase after it, hit it back…and so on and so forth. On one of these matches, I was growing rather frustrated. At the end of a long rally as I have described just now, I carefully aimed my next shot and missed, much to my disgust. And I said very quietly 'Oh damn'. My opponent chuckled as did the other spectating officers and I thought no more of it.

The next day, I was talking to a sergeant whom I barely knew in another part of the camp, when he changed the topic of conversation with a smile and said:

'I hear you said 'Oh Damn' when doing sport recently, Sir. That does not sound very Christian to me!'

He was right. But up until that point I had no idea of how making a stand for Christ in the army puts you in the spotlight, in a goldfish bowl, surrounded by a lot of guys who are just waiting for the opportunity to gleefully pounce the minute you put a foot wrong. I rapidly understood that my faith in Jesus was common knowledge across the regiment (good!). And this meant that I was being watched with interest, to see how genuine my faith was; my slightest wobble was newsworthy. That sergeant hardly knew me, and my fellow officers were not gossips, yet my slip of the tongue had generated local headlines on the bush telegraph. News of my blasphemous words had gone around the regiment like wildfire.

Now my words had been careless and wrong, but I was hardly an axe murderer. So Christians beware. We are all watched in our workplaces, because those outside the Kingdom want to see the genuineness of a Christian's walk with Jesus. The smallest slip up on the part of a Christian can allow a non-Christian to justify avoiding the call of Christ to their hearts. Now this anecdote is not to put a legalistic burden on all Christians, implying that nothing less than 100% perfection will do. We all make mistakes. However, it is important to know that how we live our lives in Christ has consequences, both intended and unintended, to our lives and beyond. It is best to walk right with Jesus and in step with the Holy Spirit.

What I learnt about living for Christ in the workplace from that unguarded moment on the squash court is true for most workplaces. Granted, soldiers are very direct and call a spade a spade, not an implement for digging. The consequences of my thoughtless words became apparent just a day later; in other workplaces where there is less transparency and more subtlety, the consequences of our careless words or actions can lie dormant for much longer. But there are consequences.

In its own way, the British Army recognises that integrity and moral uprightness is an officer-like quality. I know that may draw the odd cynical smile, but it is still expected that an officer is straight, loyal, honest and has integrity. I knew one or two that perhaps did not measure up in this area, but I knew an awful lot more that did. But the Army had a clear expectation of high standards of integrity from its officers; there were standards and not a moral vacuum.

Any officer who broke a confidence of another officer, or who was disloyal, especially in front of the sappers, could find himself a pariah very quickly. Guarding one's words became a valuable lesson and this has scriptural parallels. James 3:9-12 says about words and speech:

> 'With the tongue we praise our Lord and Father, and with it we curse human beings, who have been made in God's likeness. Out of the same mouth come praise and cursing. Can both fresh water and saltwater flow from the same spring? My brothers and sisters, can a fig-tree bear olives, or a grapevine bear figs? Neither can a salt spring produce fresh water.'

Our words are important. We cannot un-say words. Therefore, dissembling and lying in front of my fellow officers and soldiers was a definite no-no. I might add that I would not have done this anyway, I am a truthful bloke, but this aspect of my character was heavily reinforced by understanding how in line I was with officer ethics.

There were a few exceptions, of course. A very small number of my former colleagues at Sandhurst were somewhat shy of the truth in their dealings with their fellow human beings. One problem with a training establishment like Sandhurst is that fast talking can often get a person out of an awkward situation. This is fine, providing the fast talking is truthful; sadly, it is a short road from bluffing to lying. A few officer cadets followed this road that I knew of. One or two of them when caught out were told their 'services were no longer required' and exited forthwith from the Army because such behaviour was and is considered unbecoming of an officer.

Therefore, integrity is an essential hallmark of military leadership and in my opinion, any leadership. And I found it in spades at the engineer regiment. One of the OCs of one of the regimental field squadrons was (and still is) a strong Christian. He and his wife were incredibly hospitable, too. It was a great blessing to know that there was a real opportunity to grow as both a Christian and a sapper officer; this OC had been a Christian a while and so he was able to offer lots of advice, as well as fellowship. His humility and approachability spoke to me too; it reminded me afresh that there was no need to 'lord it' over subordinates as an officer. His Christian demeanour commanded respect and he was focussed without being overbearing. And it goes without saying that this OC, as a successful sapper major, represented the reality of being every inch a Christian and every inch a soldier, which was what I wanted to be.

This time in the UK, learning about how an engineer regiment works, meant that I could do something about developing other fellowship, too. So, I made an effort to get along to Officers' Christian Union weekends when they took place in the UK. This seemed like a good idea at the time and in retrospect it was great wisdom (it therefore must have been the Lord's guiding!), so I began to develop a network of fellow Christian officers. These were officers of all ages and both genders, all of whom shared a common faith in Jesus Christ.

One such officer became one of my best friends. Indeed, I was his Best Man and he was mine, but that came later; we were commissioned at the same time at Sandhurst. He was with a different training company to me and had a very different experience to me, having given his life to the Lord in the last days of his time at Sandhurst. He had been witnessed to by a fellow officer cadet during his commissioning course and made a strong profession of faith. He was to join the Royal Signals as an officer and having a similar sense of humour, we 'clicked'. For my part, it was a huge encouragement having a solid friend to whom I could be accountable before the Lord and I trust I was the same for him.

As a serving officer, I was offered the opportunity to be assigned to an OCU prayer group, which I gladly accepted. These groups, dotted up and down the country and comprising mainly retired officers and their spouses, undertook to pray regularly for the serving OCU Christians on their list. It was a growing encouragement to know that I had ongoing prayer support. I likened it to fire support, whereby a military unit is enabled to advance when the enemy's head is kept down by suppressing artillery fire. To extend this theme still further, the more specific the prayer, the better. I tried to keep my prayer group informed as to what I was doing, because concentrating your fire is far more effective in neutralising a target than random 'carpet bombing'.

This went a long way towards counteracting the sense of isolation which can really hamstring your walk with the Lord. This sense of being on your own against the world is what stopped Elijah in his tracks in 1 Kings and it can stop or slow Christians today.

The obvious antidote is church, but in the nomadic existence that is the lot of the army officer, the military Christian fellowship is the next best thing. This should not replace church of course, but at that stage I had a lot to learn about God's purposes for His church. And I often found that many Christians in churches did not really understand the military either, so this could make fellowship superficial. Many Christians I met were not convinced that a Christian should serve in the military, and while I do not recall any argument, I could tell that my military Christianity did not sit well with them. I was glad I had settled the legality of taking life issue beforehand.

This was all before the war on terror and 'Help for Heroes'. In the nineties, the main foe facing the British Army was the IRA and army personnel lived behind barbed wire, in case of IRA terrorist attacks. Military personnel were not supposed to leave base wearing military uniform, in case our cars were targeted by the IRA and consequently this created a gap between the military and civilian life. This also perpetuated the sense of ignorance about military matters amongst large sections of the British public.

Added to that was the absence of conscription in the UK and the reliance for national defence on a professional army of just over 100,000. So, most people in the UK had very little to do with the Armed Forces and consequently there was not much awareness of life in the military. This was even more the case amongst many Christians I met and I had to get used to this. It did not help my sense of isolation sometimes, but then the call of God is not always convenient.

* * * * *

I was learning a lot during my attachment at the Engineer Regiment, and it helped me to put down good Christian foundations. It went by very quickly and I began the journey of understanding the complexities of the Army, and the Royal Engineers in particular.

The sappers of the AMF(L) Field Troop were generally very good and took great pleasure in sharing their wisdom with me. I soon realised that this required a degree of filtering on my part, because occasional bias would creep into their advice and I needed to be aware of this.

They loved to regale me with their stories of run-ins with authority, and I quickly learned to weigh what they told me in this respect and not take it all at face value. So perhaps the Royal Military Police were not all vindictive, ape-like bullies after all, and may well have had just cause for locking up one or two of the sappers in the first place!

And perhaps it was just as well that one of the Corporals and his mates failed in their night time attempt to fix a large garden gnome atop the headstone of Stonehenge using ready-mix cement. Mind you, part of me rather wishes they had succeeded in their efforts to 'enhance' that pagan shrine, and that the sudden appearance of security guards and dogs had not forced their rapid retreat across the wilds of Salisbury Plain. I never did find out what happened to the gnome and the bucket of ready-mix.

That said, I loved hearing their stories and experiences. They were great soldiers and proud of being Royal Engineers. They had served all over the world and enjoyed what they did. They looked out for each other and exuded that easy camaraderie that is such a UK Armed Forces attribute. They laughed easily at and with each other, but never took themselves too seriously. Their company challenged and inspired me to be the best I could be for when my turn came to lead men like that.

I even took the Troop off to the Lake District for some adventure training. Of course, many of our vehicles were still in the UN livery, so it turned heads and caused a bit of a stir when we showed up to go hill walking. The adventure training went very well, despite one of the lorries conking out and needing major repairs.

However, the week was enlivened when a small handful of the sappers decided that a Land Rover in UN markings would really help them to attract local young women. A Land Rover is an all-terrain, four-wheel drive vehicle used extensively by the British Army (and by UK farmers) and you can easily squeeze ten people in the back of one. Knowing this, the sappers 'borrowed' one of the Land Rovers one evening to see what the 'pulling-power' of an Army Land Rover in UN markings would be in the area around Blackpool.

Well, it worked for them, as I was later to find out. But it was not just some local ladies who were attracted. The local police were somewhat interested in an Army Land Rover in UN markings, parked beneath a motorway bridge in the early hours of the morning, and investigated further.

The investigating policeman was an ex-serviceman and so had assessed the situation in seconds. He contacted the guardroom of the Training Camp where we were based and I was roused from my bed to explain why the police were calling and what exactly was one of my Land Rovers doing under a motorway bridge, crewed by an excessive number of guilty looking sappers and giggling girls?

Difficult one to answer, having just woken up after going to bed assuming all was well with the world.

To cut a long story short, it was sorted. Thankfully the sappers were not drunk, but I warned them to expect military action to be taken on returning to Salisbury Plain. The ladies were duly returned to Blackpool; I had the distinct impression that this was not their first encounter with the police. The adventure training continued. Of course, I stewed on the situation for a day or so before our return but had concluded that there was nothing I could have done about it.

At the end of the adventure training week, we all returned to Salisbury Plain, the naughty sappers to something less than a hero's welcome. I must admit to being uncertain of my culpability in this, but I was learning a big lesson that there is no shortage of potential high jinks that a soldier can get up to and that very often this is no reflection on their officer. The reaction of my fellow officers was that of amused sympathy, but no surprise, at what I had had to deal with. It was just one of those things, a good learning exercise which had been resolved, so now it was time to crack on with the next task.

This was a big encouragement to me that such matters could be closed down promptly and that life goes on. The reaction of my fellow officers was good; I had much ribbing for the 'Ladies in the Land Rover' episode, but none of it was malicious. The army employs lively young men as its sappers and soldiers; I should not be surprised if such men pushed the boundaries from time to time. After all, what do you expect of them in wartime?

My attachment was virtually over and I had thoroughly enjoyed it. I had learnt a lot about my new profession and found that I could hold my own in an officers' mess and a sapper unit. If nothing else, I recovered my self-respect and my passion for the military, which had taken a severe pounding at Sandhurst.

This was my first experience of a regular Royal Engineer regiment and it was a superb time of learning – just the tonic

I needed. I found the Royal Engineer officers to be cheerful, friendly and professional and the soldiers to be experienced and dedicated to their profession. I felt honoured to be among them and more so to be a newly commissioned officer.

The attachment helped me to grow into my rank and confirm the pathway that the Lord had chosen for me. My involvement with the OCU meant that I was less isolated spiritually, which strengthened my walk with the Lord. I had made new acquaintances and friends and was ready for the next stage of my training.

However, a gap between the end of my posting and the beginning of the next stage of my training gave me the seed of an idea to use this time to best effect.

Chapter 5 - The Escape from Las Vegas

Psalm 137:1:

'By the rivers of Babylon we sat and wept when we remembered Zion.'

For a newly commissioned army officer an attachment was a valuable time of learning, by shadowing an experienced Troop Commander without being in charge, to learn what it was like to be in charge. However, good things come to an end and the next stage of my training, the Royal Engineers Troop Commanders' Course (TCC), was coming up.

However, I had noticed that there was a gap of two weeks between the end of my attachment with the engineer regiment and the start of my engineer officer training on the TCC.

I was learning that taking the initiative was an essential military and life skill. In this case, I was aware that if I did not fill my spare fortnight with something useful, it would be filled for me. Inspecting barracks, armouries, stores and vehicles as an orderly officer may have been good military value for a junior officer like me, but it was not what I fancied doing in the summer months before a long training course. In retrospect, I am sure my fellow officers would have been delighted if I had done this work, freeing them from the more onerous aspect of their own duties. At the time, I suspected this and so I needed an alternative plan.

I had learned something of this the year before at Sandhurst, where most of the summer leave period had to be spent on 'adventure training'. This could mean an army training fortnight spent dangling on the end of a rope on a wet precipice, or force marched across Snowdonia for two weeks, whilst still being shouted at by army instructors on 'adventure training'. This would have been in the company of fellow officer cadets who had also not produced an alternative plan in time.

So, believing then (as I do now) that it is 'better to do than to be done to', I had contacted a friend of a friend. Each summer, he ran a two-week outward-bound course for Scottish borstal kids in the Inner-Hebrides. He needed an extra trained pair of hands to help him that year and I fitted the bill. The fact that it was on one of the Isles and that the course leader was ex-SAS clinched it for me in the eyes of my Sandhurst superiors, who were from Scottish Highland regiments and held UK special forces in high regard.

And to the Isles I went, whilst many of my fellow officer cadets spent the same leave period clad in Gore-Tex, clinging to granite, still being shouted at and not having escaped the military system. Meanwhile, I had a fulfilling two weeks with some fascinating teenagers, who spoke a dialect I could barely understand, far from the parade ground. I learnt survival skills, helped to shape young lives and developed a social conscience that is with me today. And I learned that when an opportunity to do something interesting presents itself, seize it with both hands.

Back to the engineer regiment. I learned that the Adjutant and the Commanding Officer (CO), the Lieutenant Colonel of the regiment, would soon be planning some activities for my spare two weeks. I strove to intercept this course of action with the flimsiest of plans, based on a conversation at a local travel agent involving cheap flights at short notice. This was the seed of the plan to avoid mundane military inspections, the outline of which I had prepared prior to visiting the CO's office.

Thus, I requested five minutes of the CO's time and respectfully mentioned that I had an opportunity for a unique budget return flight to Las Vegas, USA. I went on to add that I would appreciate seeing that part of the world for myself – there were American Indian reservations and the Grand Canyon that I wanted to see, too. I pitched it in a matter-of-fact way as befits an officer, laced with some passion because I genuinely wanted to go.

I suspect the British Army was more relaxed about things like annual leave requests than it is now and to cut a long story short, the CO agreed that this was a meaningful use of the fortnight in question. He gave me the time off to go to Las Vegas.

Looking back, I know that I had made no secret of my Christian faith whilst at the engineer regiment, and I suspect that the CO was curious to know what would happen when my faith in Christ collided with Las Vegas and its reputation. With amused largess he granted my request, asked for a postcard from Las Vegas and sent me on my way. I had taken the initiative.

Days later I was touching down in Las Vegas, the desert city looking from the air like a creation from Star Wars. Such a contrast to home, having left the damp UK spring weather for the barren brown expanse of the Nevada desert, USA. I still smile as I recall the benign shock of entering the USA for the first time, listening to people with genuine Hollywood accents, policemen with firearms and the yellow cabs. Quite a change from Salisbury Plain, England.

I caught a cab to one of the cheap B&Bs I had heard about, dropped off my luggage and went to explore 'Sin City'. What an eye opener. Nothing had prepared me for the opulence, the luxury, the extravagance of Las Vegas. Caesar's Palace, the Strip, the casino halls, the vast caverns full of fruit machines and one-armed-bandits. The desert sun and clear blue sky outside whilst the life of the city took place in a seemingly subterranean world inside.

And what a hedonistic world, of people of all shapes, sizes and backgrounds, who had arrived on vacation with their hard-earned cash with the sole intention of gambling. These punters featured the wealthy set, engaged with the roulette wheel, laughing loudly and cheerfully aware of the envious attention they were attracting. And then there were the rows of solitary gamblers putting dollar after dollar into a chosen slot machine, beside which they maintained their lonely vigil all day. These singletons were sustained by cheap burgers and coke as dollar coin by dollar coin, they emptied carrier bags containing their holiday savings. Las Vegas, far from being this glorious embodiment of the American dream, was to me a monument of vice and hedonism and not what I expected when seeking out the genuine USA. I felt as if I were in Babylon, not America, and while the rampant greed and gambling was not (and is not) to my taste it was impressive in an appalling, sickening kind of way.

However, after 24 hours of this I had had enough of Las Vegas. I was able to reflect on the CO's wry smile as he agreed my request for leave to explore. That wise old bird would have guessed I was in for a shock and wasn't he right? The question was, what was I going to do about it?

I decided it was time to leave Las Vegas and discover the USA that lay beyond. The train seemed a dull option because I was limited to the railroad. The bus lacked the flexibility and spontaneity that I wanted and so the only option to me was to hire a car. The open road, with scenery like 'Eagles' record covers (or Disney's 'Cars' and Lightning McQueen for those of you with kids) was far more appealing. It offered better prospects for adventure, and so full of hope I set off to the airport where I had seen the car hire booths when I had first arrived.

I was in for a shock. Despite having brought my driving licence, the receptionist at the first car hire booth took one look at my licence, smiled, shrugged and said:

'Sarry Sir, but ya have tah be twenny fahve to hire a carr hyer.' I was 23, two years short, and crestfallen.

I worked my way along the other car hire booths, to receive similar replies at each one. All very polite, all very sympathetic, all very consistent. Although the receptionist at one called me 'Sonny', at which I admit to bridling a little. It felt like the nativity story, with no room at any inn. A growing sense of desperation as the holiday plans seemed to be nose-diving meant that I prayed quietly, perhaps through clenched teeth, and then tried for a final time at the last booth.

I repeated my request and the same denial of opportunity was repeated to me…my heart sank. There was no point in storming off in a petulant rage as Christians shouldn't do, so I made polite conversation with the receptionist who was genuinely sympathetic; she asked me what I did for a living.

Now it so happened that being an airport-based office, this car hire booth displayed an interest in world tourism, and there were three international travel posters on its wall.

The first was headed "Come to Paris", with a classic picture of the Eifel Tower overlooking the city.

The second was headed "Come to Rome", with an impressive shot of the Colosseum in all its glory.

And the third was headed "Come to London", and it featured a row of guardsmen, in red, resplendent in bearskins, at attention with rifles and looking immaculate.

Keeping a straight face, without answering the question directly, I took from my wallet my British Army Identity Card. Dropping it carefully on her desk and pointing solemnly at the picture of the guardsmen, I said 'That's what I do.'

It was stretching things a little – I was not a member of the Foot Guards, but I had done my share of marching up and down the parade square at the Royal Military Academy, Sandhurst, being roared at by various Colour Sergeants of the Brigade of Guards. And I was definitely part of the same British Army, being a commissioned officer in the Royal Engineers for all of five months. So there.

Well, the receptionist's eyes grew to the size of saucers as she looked at me, at the poster, at my ID Card and back at me again. Her mouth lowered open like a drawbridge and about five seconds passed. Then, recovering her composure, she twittered 'Ah'll be raht bayack' and taking my ID card, scuttled out from behind her desk to the car hire booth back office, closing its door behind her.

From which came a deep bearlike series of American growls, with phrases like 'Really?', 'Yuh don't say?', 'British Arrrmy, you say?' Whereupon the door burst open and there emerged an enormous American male, a man and not the grizzly I was expecting. He was the car hire shop manager and he was huge. His arms were as big as my legs. He had a vast belly that concealed his waist belt. He had enormous sideburns like Abraham Lincoln, thick glasses like windshields and hair like a rain forest.

He looked me up and down, and his face split into an enormous grin. Reaching deep into his pocket, he drew out a set of car keys and with a wink, lobbed them to me, saying with a gravelly Southern American drawl:

'Suhn, get into thayat car, and draiiive.'

And that was that. I had a car, the paperwork and signatures completed in a twinkling and a brand-new Ford was waiting for me outside. The Grand Canyon, the open road, Navajo Indians and further American adventures beckoned. I had regained the initiative and I was free to escape from Las Vegas to discover something of the real America, which I love. I was to have one of the most enjoyable and memorable holidays of my single life, full of incident and new experience. Which will wait for another day to tell.

Meanwhile, back in Las Vegas, exhaling my thank you to the Lord, I got into that car and drove.

And I remembered to send the CO a postcard.

Chapter 6 - Learning to build...The Troop Commanders' Course

Proverbs 15:14:

'The discerning heart seeks knowledge, but the mouth of a fool feeds on folly.'

On my return from the USA, it was time to start the Troop Commanders' Course, or TCC. This was a training course designed to equip future Royal Engineers Troop Commanders with all the skills necessary to command their troop of 30 sappers.

The TCC took about eight months' and covered the whole range of military engineering aspects that a Troop Commander was likely to encounter. As I have described in a previous chapter, the range of tasks undertaken by the Royal Engineers was and is very broad, and so the TCC had to cover as much of these aspects as possible.

Therefore, the topics ranged from how to run a construction site, to health and safety, to all aspects of military engineering. Throughout the TCC, the balance being struck was to give the officer the training to deliver his or her role, whilst understanding something of what the sappers would have to do to deliver that role as well. This was to help the officer be realistic in what he or she expected of their future Field Troop.

For the TCC, us 'Troopys', as us sapper Field Troop Commanders were called, were there to learn the recce and project management skills necessary for us and our future Field Troops to deliver combat engineer and construction tasks.

The course was based in Chatham, in Kent, which is the Headquarters of the Royal Engineers. The tempo was a world away from Sandhurst; we were treated like adults and expected to behave that way. The quote at the beginning of the chapter sums up the sense of making the most of a course like this to be in the best position to hit the ground running when I reached my Field Troop as its commander!

My fellow 'Troopys' were a good bunch and we were quite a relaxed TCC. Many of the guys had been Corporals in the Royal Engineers before being selected for officer training and that was a real benefit to the rest of us. It meant that there was a lot of experience already amongst us on the TCC, which led to better understanding of the combat engineer principles.

We started by learning about construction work, then moved onto the combat engineer skills we would need. I found my very theoretical academic civil engineer degree to be of surprisingly limited use. Also, I had specialised in geo-technical engineering and alas there was little need for Royal Engineer Troop Commanders to design dams. In retrospect, I would have been better specialising in structural engineering! The only usage of dams by Royal Engineers as far as I could tell was as a mild form of swearing, as I had learnt back at the engineer regiment during my attachment.

The TCC also spent time learning about plant – diggers, graders, excavators, dozers and the like, of which the Royal Engineers possesses a surprisingly large number. Learning how long it takes a pair of medium wheel tractors to excavate a 'tank slot' from which a Challenger Main Battle Tank can fire is suddenly very important when the Battlegroup Commander is pressing the sapper officer to know how quickly his tanks can engage the enemy.

Learning to calculate planning times such as this was a key aspect of the course. Engineer tasks take time and the commander to whom the sapper officer is reporting needs to know how long a minefield will take to clear or how long a bridge will take to build or how long it will take to set up a bridge for demolition. The Royal Engineers produce excellent aide-memoires to summarise these facts, all of which are impossible to remember.

Thus, when the course moved onto battlefield engineering, it became very interesting. This is because executing these battlefield combat engineering tasks successfully would make all the difference as to whether the battlegroup could live, move and fight and prevent the enemy from doing the same.

This large phase was divided into modules, such as bridging, mine warfare, demolitions and so on. The training on each module was led by an experienced Captain Instructor and a Quartermaster Sergeant Instructor, or QMSI for short. They were addressed as 'Q'. Nothing to do with James Bond.

A 'Q' was a Warrant Officer Second Class, the same rank as a Squadron Sergeant Major. I had met my first 'Q' as a lad, when as a TA officer my Dad had been visited at our home by a Royal Engineers QMSI to plan some TA training. What was memorable was that Dad had told Mum that Q Leigh was coming over and could we have one more to supper. Mum, not being over familiar with army ranks, assumed it was a Chinese engineer from Dad's office in the Department of Transport. Imagine her surprise when a six-foot strapping white Caucasian sapper appeared at the front door and not the

'Qu Lee' she was expecting. That incident generated a lot of giggles at Dad's TA unit.

I also knew of a Staff Sergeant Coomber, who then became a QMSI on promotion...and henceforth raised a laugh every time he introduced himself by his rank. I am sure he was always a cool character, but I bet introducing himself as a cucumber meant he couldn't wait to get the next promotion.

These men were SNCOs of great experience. Most had been Troop Staff Sergeants and knew combat engineering inside out; some of them had been doing it for twenty years.

For our next phase of the TCC we learnt all about bridging, or 'Gap Crossing in the Combat Zone', one of the key roles of the Royal Engineers.

For readers unfamiliar with this, I cannot stress enough how physical Combat Engineer bridging is. One of the key tasks of the Royal Engineers in peace or war is to provide a means by which the rest of the army can cross a gap and it is a risky undertaking. Royal Engineer equipment bridges must be built quickly, often by hand because it is quicker and more reliable. This is because in war, there is usually an aggressive enemy on the opposite side of the gap who does not want the bridge to be built.

There is a graphic picture in the Royal Engineers Headquarters Officers' Mess in Brompton Barracks in Chatham called 'Bridging the Rapido' by Terence Cuneo, which depicts Royal Engineers building a Bailey Bridge under accurate enemy fire in Italy during World War Two. It vividly shows the urgency, danger and hard physical nature of building an equipment bridge, in this case across the River Rapido, in the combat zone.

It is the job of the Troop Commander to plan and design the bridge and that of the Troop Staff Sergeant, the Staffy, to control the construction of the bridge itself. The rest of the Troop would be divided into its sections, each commanded by a Corporal, as 'left of bridge', 'right of bridge' and 'centre of bridge' for the construction of the equipment bridge.

All the component parts of an equipment bridge must be portable by hand and so are described as 'two-man-lift', or 'four-man-lift', etc. It is like an enormous Meccano model. The bridge is then assembled in a strict sequence on the friendly side of the gap and then 'boomed' out across the divide, a few metres at a time, on rollers. No more than half of the bridge at a time can be 'boomed out', or else it can over balance on the rollers and fall into the gap. Which is difficult and time consuming to extract and not good for the morale of the builders. Bridges can range in size from a few yards to hundreds of yards, depending upon the gap size. Irrespective of its size you can see that there are a lot of 'four-man', 'six-man' and 'eight-man' lifts in an equipment bridge of any size and get an idea of the hard work involved in assembling it. This also means that there are no weaklings serving in Royal Engineers field troops; sappers take their physical fitness very seriously.

As Troop Commanders, we had the opportunity to build the Medium Girder Bridge, which was the standard Royal Engineer equipment bridge at that time; and satisfying hard work it was too. But on operations, that was not the Troop Commander's role; our role was to recce the gap and, based largely on its width and the load bearing strength of the bank on either side, decide the size of bridge needed and plan its construction.

The next phase was demolitions, which was a boy's dream come true. The live explosives training culminated in a 'Dems Day', where we all got to blow up large pieces of junk and a couple of old cars on the range on the Isle of Sheppey in Kent.

Very satisfying seeing these items blown up in the air, and then scant seconds later hearing the 'krump, krump' of the explosions as the sound reached us.

We had instruction on how to plan a bridge demolition, first by classifying the bridge and then determining how to blow it up so that it was as difficult as possible for an enemy to repair and/or re-use. To this day, whenever I see a bridge, I still like to work out how I would demolish it!

Our training using dummy explosives (plasticine) culminated in rigging one of the bridges over the Medway River in Rochester with fake explosive as a practice demolition. The Royal School of Military Engineering has an agreement with the local authorities to do this from time to time as a training exercise, providing it is done overnight to minimise disruption; the bridge is closed during the exercise. I say 'has'; I presume this is still the case. This was probably a Health and Safety nightmare for the Instructor and the QMSI, with a load of us yahooing officers wanting to swarm all over the bridge, excitedly fixing plasticine in all the right places so that the bridge was effectively ready to be blown up. The plasticine was a lurid blue colour, to ensure it was never mistaken for the white plastic explosive that we actually used to blow up things.

As ever, lighter moments happened. In the build-up to the night demolition exercise on Rochester Bridge, the TCC was given much instruction on how different shapes of explosive could achieve different things. So, we spent a few hours moulding the plasticine into various shapes to perform different theoretical acts of demolition when detonated. This was all under the watchful and approving gaze of the QMSI, together with an American Master Sergeant who was with the Royal School of Military Engineering on exchange.

With the lesson drawing to a close, the QMSI told us to stop what we were doing in order to get the plasticine back into its original shape, ready for the next course after us. At this point, one of the coarser members of the TCC offered to do it all on behalf of the TCC while the rest of us went for a tea break. Surprised, yet appreciative of his largess, we all left the site and grabbed a cup of tea before the end of the day while our fellow TCC member packed all the plasticine into the boxes in its original shape.

Or so we thought.

What this cheeky chappie had done was to mould all the lumps of blue plasticine into various sizes of male genitilia, and then pack them into the boxes to surprise the next course of combat engineers. The rows of boxes, with their revolting cobalt blue phallic contents, looked like a delivery to a rather vulgar modern art exhibition.

The QMSI had been suspicious, rather than surprised, of the officer's kind offer to pack the plasticine away and had gone back to check. The QMSI, on examining the officer's handiwork and very familiar with the childish ways of young Royal Engineer officers, merely rolled his eyes and shook his head. The American Master Sergeant, perhaps far less familiar with this childish expression of this brand of humour so prevalent across the British Army, was just speechless.

And I cannot for the life of me remember if the plasticine was left in situ, or re-packed properly.

On a more serious note, the TCC was designed to heighten our understanding of the battlefield on which Royal Engineers are expected to exert considerable influence. The application on the battlefield for much of this training was wrapped up in a series of Tactical Exercises without Troops, or TEWTs. This was where we were taken to an area of countryside and told to imagine that a certain number of enemy battlegroups were attacking from the east and that we as Troop Commanders had to plan the defence of the following grid squares. We were told how many sappers and tractors/dozers/diggers we had at our disposal. We were told what our battlegroup commander wanted to achieve. And then we set to and planned the defence.

We learned that trees, trenches, mines and barbed wire may slow a determined enemy, but would not stop him. We learned that it was better to channel an enemy into a killing area for the battlegroup, so it was essential that we knew what weapons, orbat and deployment a battlegroup has. This made the defence plan more effective. We learned something of the likely enemy equipment. So, if a well armoured enemy tank was forced to jink from side to side by intelligent defence works, then one of our anti-tank weapons could engage the flank of the tank, which is less well protected. We learned to incorporate the terrain into the battle plan, so that it enhanced the defence. And if sufficient Royal Engineers' earth moving plant equipment was available, then we knew we could alter the terrain to suit the plan too.

I loved TEWTs because as a Royal Engineers Troop Commander you had to understand the bigger picture and your essential part in it. Which is exactly what we must do as Christians. We must understand what our great Captain of the Heavenly Host, Jesus Christ, is doing across a much bigger zone than we ourselves occupy. We must understand our part in His plan and faithfully do it. Perhaps most difficult for some of us, we must trust others in the same army as us to do their allocated task, and get on with completing our own allocated tasks without getting distracted by advising others on what they should be doing. Sound familiar?

It is that sense of everyone having a vital yet different role to play, whilst all being soldiers, that is such an attractive aspect of the military life. And it should be no different for Christians.

One of the features that hones teamwork in the British Army is the constant reminder that you are training to fight an enemy, from whom you can expect no mercy. This develops teamwork, sometimes called covenant, watching each other's backs and working together until everyone's task is done.

I wonder if us Christians forget how vindictive and cruel our enemy Satan is, and that perhaps his favourite way to get at the Lord is by harming us. Jesus is very clear in John 10:10:

> *'The thief comes only to steal and kill and destroy;*
> *I have come that they may have life, and have it*
> *to the full.'*

The 'thief' is Satan, who is not a nice little devil. Just our being more aware of this would make for better cohesion amongst Christians; we find it easy to squabble amongst ourselves, or to blame the Lord if things don't go according to plan (whose plan?). But there is a being who, with his demonic minions, is literally hell-bent on wrecking our lives. How often do we take the battle to him? Isn't that part of abundant life in all its fullness?

I am not saying focus on the devil; after all he is a failed worship leader who wanted all the glory, so we don't give him undue attention, but Jesus also says in Matthew 18:18:

> *'Truly I tell you, whatever you bind on earth will be*
> *bound in heaven,*
> *and whatever you loose on earth will be loosed in*
> *heaven.'*

So, we have been given authority to do something about it, rather than merely endure it. I say 'we' because wars are not won by individual actions. The Lord wants us Christians to work together, just as He, the Father and the Holy Spirit are in perfect unity as they work together for our good.

The British Army (and any decent army) works well together because it is trained to; there is a strong sense of military discipline to discourage the work-shy and because the British Army usually has an enemy to think about at some time. Since the Second World War, I believe there has only been one year that no British soldier was killed on operations somewhere.

The other aspect I want to introduce in this book to encourage Christians is that the British Army, irrespective of mistakes it makes in battle, does end up winning its wars and this is quite a track record. There is a certain amount of truth in the statement that it produces some of the finest, bravest soldiers on the planet. I agree, but other armies have brave soldiers as well.

However, there is a statement regarding the British soldier (and sapper) that I once read and have never forgotten. With regards the British soldier, *no other soldier on earth has as much confidence in the courage of the soldier standing next to him.*

That speaks to me powerfully of team, of utter mutual respect, reliability and the knowledge of having your back covered. This must be a hallmark of Christians and the church, Jesus' church that He is returning to claim as His bride. The question is always, *are we a pure and spotless bride that is ready for Him?*

That seems quite a digression from describing the Troop Commanders' Course, but a necessary one.

I found my fellow officers quite interested in Christianity, though one or two were hostile. No matter, they were all professional and we got on reasonably well. However, I can think of one occasion when I divided opinion amongst my peers. It was when a female potential officer spent a lunchtime with the TCC to find out more about the Royal Engineers. She was bright and pleasant but did not match the stereotype Alpha-female for whom so many of my (all male) fellow officers yearned. Generally speaking, they ignored her. I felt this was discourteous and so I took it upon myself to host her, despite the nudges, because otherwise she would have been left on her own and that reflected badly on the unit.

After she left, I weighed up whether to let it go or say something. I felt it right to say something, so before our next lesson and while the TCC was together I stood at the front of the classroom and pointed out that in my opinion the TCC had been rude and let itself down by ignoring the lady. I spelt out my suspicions why and said I hoped we'd do better in future. Well, that got a reaction! Most of it positive, by the way, with comments such as 'point taken'. But some felt I had completely exceeded my remit and were most indignant. If we make a stand as Christians, we may distance some friends, but I sincerely believe we gain respect from others; they see that Jesus' values are real to you and people need to see that if they are to be saved. Mind you, I could have been more gracious, but on reflection my blunt approach did get the message across.

The TCC continued apace, with lessons on route reconnaissance, watermanship (the Royal Engineers have responsibility for freshwater boating), so those of the TCC with webbed feet were happy. We also learned about water supply, to provide drinkable water for up to a brigade (2000 soldiers) from a muddy, contaminated water source.

Weekends were generally clear and so most of us left the base on Friday afternoon. I could spend time with friends and strengthen links with the OCU. I went home to the South West of course, where my Dad as an ex-sapper officer was keen to subtly grill me about the training I had received.

As a course, we became involved with officer duties at the Royal School of Military Engineering, which meant taking turns to serve as Orderly Officer for the base. This was essentially being the first point of contact for any unusual situations, especially during the silent hours. That would include inspecting the guard for the base (which meant your turnout had to be at least as good as theirs) and inspecting prisoners.

Prisoners were soldiers who had fallen foul of military law and it had been judged by the CO that they needed to 'do time' to atone for whatever military misdemeanour they had committed. The cells were in the guardroom and prisoners were kept busy by the Guard Commander doing chores and cleaning, in case they ever got the idea that being in jail was better than doing their normal duties. The crimes varied from significant drunkenness to being absent without leave (AWOL).

One prisoner that I remember was a soldier who had brought a young lady onto the base and once there they had decided to become better acquainted. Unfortunately, they had been rather noisy about becoming more amorous towards each other, and the idyllic piece of parkland shrubbery where they had chosen to develop their friendship happened to be the Commandant's garden. He was not amused and so the sapper ended up doing time in the Guardroom cells. I don't recall him being particularly repentant.

It was good talking with the Guard Commanders, usually experienced Corporals or Sergeants, who were seasoned sappers. They appreciated being asked for their advice and I did not have to apply the filter very often. And they loved recounting funny stories of their high jinks.

The best one was about the grand statue of General Gordon of Khartoum, which is located just inside the Royal School of Military Engineering by the main gate. It is very obvious and is one of the first objects a visitor beholds on entering the base. General Gordon was a renowned Royal Engineer officer of the Victorian era, who made his name first in China and then in Sudan. He was famously killed at the conclusion of the Siege of Khartoum in 1885 and died a national hero. By the way, he was a noted Christian of his time and it is worth looking him up.

But on with the story.

The statue is of General Gordon, astride a camel depicting how he looked when he served in Egypt and Sudan. At some point, some nameless, mischievous Royal Engineer made the discovery that this statue was hollow, made of metal and therefore watertight. The fact that the camel was clearly a male camel and the proximity of the Guardroom firehose allowed a plan to be formed. At some point, and no-one knows (or will admit) when, the statue was filled up with water from the Guardroom fire hose. And still no one noticed.

Once this was done, the nameless, mischievous Royal Engineer obtained a cordless drill with a narrow drill bit no more than 2mm in diameter that could drill through metal. Very easy to obtain in the Royal School of Military Engineering, which as well as Troop Commanders also trains all the sapper tradesmen, artisans, welders and construction engineers for the Royal Engineers. The said tool was easy to 'borrow'. Then at the dead of night, when no one, not even the Orderly

Officer was around, a hole was drilled into the protruding end of the camel's metallic male member.

Whereupon a thin, yet very visible stream of water appeared… and so it streamed for days, as the almost life-sized hollow statue slowly decanted the large volume of water stored within through the 2mm hole. This seemingly perpetually urinating camel caused a mixture of amusement and embarrassment to Royal Engineers and visitors alike and the incident has gone down in Royal Engineers folklore.

The TCC was nearly at an end and we all received posting orders to our Engineer Regiments and our first Troop Commander appointments. Mine was to an Engineer Regiment in Germany, of a similar organisation (or Order of Battle – Orbat) to the one where I had spent a good attachment earlier that year.

I was pleased. Germany was an exciting destination. I speak reasonable German, it was somewhere new and was viewed as something of a centre of excellence for combat engineering.

Those of us heading to similar engineer regiments were booked into the Royal Engineers Armoured Vehicles Course, which was based at the Royal Armoured Corps main UK training area in Bovington, Dorset. It was one of the most enjoyable courses I have been on, accurately described as 'two weeks squeezed into four'. It was surprisingly valuable. Up to that point, going to war for me meant marching there and carrying your kit; hopefully, there might be the chance of a lift from a lorry. Going to war in your own tank meant relative comfort. You had a means of keeping warm with an engine and in German winters that was a considerable plus point. As one well-bred Challenger Tank commander put it to me:

'Mark, tanks are marvellous. I go to war in a tank weighing 60 tonnes; 50 tonnes of it is my personal kit.'

Now I never got to that extreme, but it was good to know I did not have to carry everything on my back in future.

The purpose of the course was to familiarise us with the tracked vehicles we would use in our future field troops.

This meant the Spartan light tank, the Combat Vehicle Reconnaissance (Tracked) or CVR(T) to give it its official name for us Troop Commanders. This was a petrol driven tank which had just a driver and commander. Its purpose was to get the recce officer (i.e. me) across the battlefield quickly. On the plus side, it carried a General-Purpose Machine Gun, or GPMG in its small manually operated turret and could hit speeds of 70mph on the flat with a following wind. This was not recommended across country because it made for a very bumpy ride. Its drawback from my perspective was that I, the commander, stood on its petrol tank.

The other armoured vehicle used in the field troops was the 432, which was an armoured personnel carrier. It was also called a 'pack'. In other words, a metal box on tracks, which was crewed by a driver and commander (either the Troop Staff Sergeant or a Section Commander) and had room for up to ten sappers in the back. The 432 was the doyen of Armoured Fighting Vehicles (AFVs) in the British Army, and had been designed in the 1950s based on World War Two German AFVs! I gather it is still in service having had an upgrade. Back in the nineties it was notoriously slow compared to the Challenger and Warrior AFVs used by the tank and infantry battlegroups respectively. However, it was rugged, simple and semi-reliable and generally liked by its sapper crews.

The course also gave us opportunity to look at the armoured engineers, who drove big tanks with folding bridges and all sorts of other kit stored on the top. They were much bigger vehicles, using the former British Army Chieftain Tank chassis without the original 120mm gun as a platform for carrying these enormous folding bridges which could span a gap of many metres. Other uses were to carry fascines (bundles of metal pipes to drop into a gap to cross it) or other assault gear. The Armoured Royal Engineers who operated these vehicles had a different role to field engineers, which was to cross a narrowish gap quickly. But in a wartime situation we would work together; for example, sappers from a Field Troop would be checking the enemy side of a gap for any land mines before the folding bridge was placed in position.

We also viewed the tank driving simulator, which was one of the legacies of the cold war that was still very much in use at the Royal Armoured Corps Training Centre. It was an enormous room, containing a massive scale model of a German landscape, with authentic looking villages, forest and fields. It looked like one of those electric model train sets that railway enthusiasts own, which has the little trains steaming through an exact scale landscape to make the model railway as true to life as possible. The simulator itself predated CGI and computer animation, having been built many years before. It featured all the controls, dials and pedals that you would find in the driver's compartment in a tank and was an exact replica of where the driver would sit, to make it 100% realistic.

The two were connected by a huge camera with a tiny lens at ground level on the model landscape, which was suspended on a gantry with rollers above the scale model. What the camera saw through its view finder was exactly the same as the driver's view from the tank. Especially so if the driver was being trained to drive using only his periscopes for vision in the 'battened down' state. This was the only view that the driver in the simulator was allowed, to make it realistic.

The aim of the simulator was to give tank drivers experience of hazardous driving without causing untold damage to people, property, tanks and tank crews. The prospect of the camera accidentally nudging the side of a scale model building was a much safer and more cost-effective option for correcting driver error. The alternative scenario when training any new tank driver is the risk of a mistake causing a 60-tonne tank to end up in the living room of an occupied family home.

While it seems dated now, and now there is probably a computer-generated set of graphics replicating any terrain and scenario on the planet, it worked well for its time. Our instructors told us that once drivers settled into it, the simulator was very realistic for them and many forgot they were driving through a model set. The training value would then be increased by hiding scale models of Russian made tanks, usually the ubiquitous T-72, in various places so that tank drivers began to think about how to reduce the risk of ambush and observing their routes more carefully.

One of the instructors told us that a while back, to liven things still further, he had caught a large garden spider the night before he led a simulator training day with some tank drivers.

During of one of the next simulator sessions, a highly-strung trainee tank driver was carefully inching his way through the scale model German village, on red alert for a hidden T-72 ambush. Suddenly, round the street corner appeared not the T-72 ambush he anticipated, but an enormous hairy alien creature, with ferocious eyes and great legs, towering over the houses as it strode down the street towards him. The tank driver, who was completely 'in the zone', uttered the most unmanly howl of terror as he beheld the monstrous, hideous horror that approached him.

The rest of his course, who had been tipped off and now gathered to watch the unfolding spectacle, collapsed in hysterics. What had happened was that the instructor had released his trapped spider onto the scale model, and from the camera's perspective a spider a few centimetres across assumed the scale dimensions of a large dinosaur, but much more animated. The British Army and its sense of humour are seldom parted.

The course highlight for me was the training to operate the turret of a Spartan whilst firing the GPMG at targets seemingly miles away on Lulworth ranges. The noise was deafening and firing these tracer rounds, which streaked away from the GPMG across the moorland for 2km before hammering the old tank hulk targets was fantastic.

Thus, the Royal Engineers Armoured Vehicle course concluded, and as that door shut so the next one opened. The real work was about to start and with my worldly goods loaded into my Renault 11, I set off to Northern Germany to my first posting as a Troop Commander, to a proper field engineer regiment that undertook field engineering, and a fresh adventure.

Chapter 7 - Welcome to Germany

Proverbs 17:28-29:

'The one who has knowledge uses words with restraint, and whoever has understanding is even-tempered. Even fools are thought wise if they keep silent, and discerning if they hold their tongues.'

Germany was a fantastic year of experiences. Some of these were good, some of these were not so enjoyable at the time, but all of them were valuable life lessons.

Being based away from the UK brought its own challenges. In UK regiments, officers and soldiers tried to get away to be with friends and family when they were off duty and seldom frittered away a weekend on the base. In Germany, with the UK nearly 12 hours away by car (and northern and western Britain even further), there was much more of a social life within the regiment because most people preferred to stay on base rather than spend money to be travelling the whole weekend. This made for an interesting change to my army life so far.

The regiment was based in an old German Army barracks in a typical, spotless, north German town set amongst flat farmland and forests.

There were two field squadrons and a large support squadron in the regiment. The support squadron looked after engineer stores like bridging, as well as holding a considerable quantity of earth moving equipment. There was a headquarters squadron, too, because in wartime the regiment supported more than just the three squadrons.

The barracks was quite big, with large three storey accommodation blocks for each squadron, which were of solid German construction. The three storeys were accommodation for the single sappers and corporals, with the troop offices and troop stores being housed in the basement. In the loft area was the squadron bar, which was a focal point for squadron social life.

I was posted as a Field Troop Commander in one of the field squadrons and this is the squadron I will focus on for my narrative, because it was my bread and butter for the duration.

The squadron was in a state of flux following its recent return from one of the first 'Operation Grapple' tours of duty in the Former Republic of Yugoslavia. This was at the time when the British Army was being deployed to Bosnia as part of the UN-backed peace keeping operations in the early nineties, and wherever the British Army is in any numbers, there will always be its sappers. 'Operation Grapple' was the army code name for this deployment. I was to become very familiar with the term 'Operation Grapple' in later months. The squadron also had quite a reputation for the lively behaviour of its sappers, of which, more later.

I decided from the outset that I would not attempt to dazzle my new troop with my brilliance and that the proverb quoted at the start of this chapter was a good place to start. I knew I had one mouth and a pair of ears. My new troop was made up of very seasoned sappers and a staff sergeant who was due for posting in a matter of weeks. I was the newest one there, untested, and they knew it.

But you must start somewhere and so it was time to meet my new troop, the army way, on parade. It was my job to inspect them on my first Monday morning in the cold German winter. It is a unique experience, meeting your first command as a junior officer. I daresay every officer remembers that moment. It is not a one-way inspection either, I was aware that the scrutiny was being returned. They want to know what kind of 'Troopy' they are getting. Are they a leader? Are they a liability? Are they harsh? Are they approachable? Are they willing to listen? Can they make decisions? Will I get an easy life? And so on.

Well, time would tell for answers to their questions. My new troop seem well turned out and of suitable soldierly bearing. Alas, I was soon to learn that field troops are generally near full strength for operations and key exercises, but can rapidly dwindle in between times. Reasons for this were training courses, especially in a skilled organisation like the Royal Engineers which takes its refresher training seriously. I mentioned before that many were overdue posting, which didn't help. Added to all of this was an increase in IRA activity, which meant more sappers from the field troops were required for guard duty than ever before. Also, when I arrived the senior Troop Commander in the squadron was taking his field troop on a big British Army training exercise in Canada, or BATUS as it is known. That meant his troop was augmented by sappers from mine and the other field troop.

Finally, the British Armed Forces' scheme for reducing its size in the early nineteen nineties, 'Options for Change', was beginning to bite and this led to a further exodus of experienced corporals, sergeants and senior sappers. Many of these sappers were actually reluctant to leave, but the redundancy packages being offered were very generous. Sappers are very employable people and so those who were able to secure a good job on leaving, with a five-figure sum in their back pocket, reckoned they would never have this opportunity again. All too often I heard the phrase 'I don't want to leave, but I would be mad to ignore this offer!'

So in a few months, I had no Staff Sergeant, one Corporal and a handful of sappers in my troop, which was a frustrating state of affairs. Many of the squadron officers and SNCOs were posted too, with gaps between their replacements arriving, which didn't help!

I penned a few silly lines of poetry which summed up the frustration from a Troop Commander's perspective of trying to make a field troop work with a handful of sappers, because kit maintenance, routine training and a whole host of other duties still had to carry on as before. My two fellow squadron Field Troop Commanders heartily endorsed it:

> No more men, all are on guard,
> Or out in BATUS working hard,
> Or adventure training in the sun-kissed med,
> With someone else's Troop instead.
>
> Day in the office, piles of paper,
> Try the phone, what a caper,
> No one in to answer questions,
> On what's required for the next inspection.
>
> Scrub the floor, paint the packs,
> Office tidy, shelves all stacked,
> And soundly bolted to the wall,
> Health and safety in case they fall.
>
> The job's OK despite the groan,
> The Troop is yours, you're on your own,
> Even if the Troop's just three strong,
> You're the Boss, chaps carry on…

However, before that hit home, we did deploy on a two-week exercise on the large Soltau training area in northern Germany. This training area was a bleak, undulating yet featureless expanse of heathland many miles across. In mid-winter, covered in wet army vehicle ruts and under leaden skies, with no vegetation and its remaining brown grass laced with sleet, Soltau was no tourist destination. Most of my sappers knew it well, having trained there many, many times before.

The first week was an intensive squadron combat engineering exercise, which was really good and my first opportunity to put my training into practice. It was mid-winter, after a lot of rain followed by frost and heavy snow. I was very happy to be doing my job in a Spartan light tank rather than on foot or even in a Land Rover.

At last I was part of a combat engineering unit, in the field, doing what I had wanted to do for so long. For me and the other Troop Commanders, it was a series of recces for engineering tasks, I recall mine including a minefield and a bridge, which our field troops would then build. Obviously, it was a dummy minefield, not a real one, built using either biodegradable dummy mines or heavy plastic ones which had to be dug up after the exercise and cleaned and stored for the next.

As ever, sleep was at a premium on such exercises. Recces require a lot of walking the ground, thinking the task through and calculating the resources (sappers, stores, plant, other assets) and timings required. Then checking that I had done what I had been tasked to do by the OC. In between doing that, it was important that I checked that the task of my last recce was progressing on time, and that I had some time to gauge how the field troop was doing with the Troop Staff Sergeant and the sappers themselves. Food and cups of tea were important, too. And the occasional quiet time with the

Lord, with mini NIV Bible in hand, sitting on the engine louvers to keep warm, to the wry amusement of my guys. So sleep had to fit around that.

In the middle of that mad week, a Sergeant from the REME support unit for our squadron trundled past me in his 432 Armoured Fighting Vehicle. His REME unit was responsible for maintenance of our vehicles and equipment beyond what we could do ourselves. He stopped beside me and leant down from his lofty perch as he beheld me hacking on foot through the muddy snow recceing the next task, notebook in hand, rifle on shoulder, wearing webbing and looking determined.

'I tell you what, Sir,' he grinned through the flurries of snow 'I would not do that job of yours for all the money in the world!'

Well, fine for him to say, but amazingly, I was enjoying it. By the end of the week, we were so worn out that the Ops Officer virtually fell asleep giving his own orders and the Squadron Sergeant Major described us Troop Commanders as being 'grey' with fatigue.

But it had gone well. The OC was pleased, which is always a bonus for a Troop Commander.

The next week my field troop stayed put to support a Brigade exercise on the same training area – we were called 'Neutral Org' and not participating in the exercise. Instead, I was required to set up fake minefields, bridge crossings and obstacles using white tape so that the Brigadier's herd of tanks had to do some thinking about the routes they chose instead of ploughing across the training area in an unrealistic straight line between its objectives. I was also tasked to set up some battlefield simulations, or 'batsims' for short, at specific sites to liven up the exercise for his battlegroups.

A batsim is where explosives are laid during a training exercise, usually to simulate enemy fire. There is quite an art to it. Often, it is a series of medium charges in a marked off area the size of a sports pitch, which go off individually to replicate an enemy artillery bombardment. Or a piece of detonation cord attached to a smaller charge can simulate a rocket attack. And so on.

So, the Brigadier and his exercise training entourage set out in their respective armoured vehicles across Soltau to decide where things were going to happen. I had noticed that many senior officers can appear quite relaxed about where they want things to take place, and then be rather upset when they don't go exactly to plan. The featureless nature of Soltau, with the snow, meant that I could not guarantee finding again the exact spot to which the Brigadier was languidly gesticulating. I solved this by bringing a 432 full of sappers with me, complete with metal pickets and white tape. Every time the Brigadier outlined the next phase, decided upon his obstacle and looked at me, I called the 432 forward and out piled a handful of cheery sappers to mark the locations of his obstacles or batsims as we made our progress across the plain.

Then the field troop and I stayed out on Soltau for the exercise, to make sure everything was in order. It was good to spend time with my guys, many of whom were being posted, but who had interesting lives. It was cold, though, with thick snow on the ground and temperatures dropping to minus ten. This is where armoured vehicles are much better than army ponchos at keeping the cold out, and the food warm.

On one of those frosty nights I took my Spartan to check one of the obstacles. It was bitterly cold, yet very still, with a full moon. The snow reflected the moonlight so sharply that you could see for miles across the Soltau plain. It was a fantastic time to be outdoors in such ethereal weather conditions which do not really occur in the UK. Added to that was the bonus of commanding a tank from atop its turret, which I never stopped enjoying.

One of the Corporals had come along for the ride and he noticed some tracks in the snow in the moonlight just beside us. As we were not 'fighting' in the exercise, I could justify switching on the spotlight in the Spartan's small turret to investigate; had we been on the exercise, I would have been guilty of giving away my position and being 'eliminated'. I wanted to look closer without having to jump down from the Spartan.

Just as well. The tracks were fresh and they were of a large family of wild boar, making their way across the training area. And the makers of tracks were only two hundred yards further on. We followed this boar family across the frozen waste for a few miles, all of us chuckling at and enjoying the experience of an unexpected winter safari. I am not sure whether it would catch on, but an armoured Spartan CVR(T) is a much more sensible mobile vantage point for viewing potentially dangerous wildlife like my old friends the hippo and the elephants, than some of these thin safari vehicles that you see on the films. But I suppose fleets of Spartans grinding up and down the Serengeti might be a little more expensive in fuel, and it might not leave much of the Savannah.

Another interesting event for me took place the following evening. The exercise was now on, and the batsims were to go off the following day as planned. The weather had closed in from the previous clear conditions and it was now foggy, with poor visibility and windy flurries of snow. I had placed the Spartan near one group of batsims and far away across Soltau, my Staff Sergeant was near the other batsims site. Each site was marked with white tape and illuminous glow sticks for night-time use. Just the two bombardments for the Brigade to endure in the morning.

NEHEMIAH IN THE NINETIES

It was dead of night and my sappers and I were snoozing in the Spartan. Whereupon I awoke to the sensation of rumbling. It was not my stomach and I am a very heavy sleeper. What was this rumbling? It was reminiscent of that sequence in the film 'Dances with Wolves', where the first inkling of the arrival of the buffalo herd is awareness of the ground shaking.

This was happening now.

Tanks! And they were heading our way. Without thinking and as the rest of the sappers were stirring, I piled out of my sleeping bag, grabbed a torch, conscious that a load of explosives was laid out nearby, ready for the morning. The rumbling was growing much louder and it was heading straight for the batsims.

I stumbled out of the Spartan and ran through the snow to where the batsims were sited. I was just in time for the first tanks to crest the low ridge near the edge of the area where we had set the explosives. I stood at the edge of the batsim area, waved the torch, shouting 'Stop!' at the top of my voice. To no avail.

Fifty plus tonnes of Challenger tank can move very quickly. It was dark, snowing and foggy and these lumbering steel beasts were not hanging around. They were throwing up a lot of muddy snow as they did so. I doubt if the drivers or commanders could even see the batsim area or its markers before they crashed straight through it. They certainly did not see or hear me.

I found myself having to desperately side-step several of the Challengers as they rapidly loomed out of the darkness and roared past. Tanks are no respecter of flesh and blood. If I had timed it wrongly, I would have been strawberry jam in the snow, with the odd piece of torch and army uniform added. My goodness me, I was wide awake now.

Then as quickly as it had started, it was over. As the noise of the last of the Challengers disappeared into the darkness and I stood panting, recovering my breath and composure, the sappers joined me.

'Glad yis are stull with us, Sor!' said one of the Scottish sappers.

My unthinking action had been very rash, because laying down one's life for a set of inert explosives (we had thankfully not fitted the detonators, preferring to do that at the last minute) is not a clever thing to do. Even with the remote possibility of one of the charges going off, it would not have made any dent in a Challenger. But a Challenger would have made quite a dent in me.

'Ah suspect yis'll no be doin that agin, Sor!' grinned the Corporal, another Scotsman, when he saw I was alright.

The Lord definitely had His hand on me that night.

We inspected the damage. All the wires and explosives were hideously tangled; a fast-moving cavalry squadron group of 14 Challengers does not leave a smooth wake.

Well, we disentangled wire from explosive and set it all up again in time for the morning. As a footnote, when it came to detonate at the specified time the following morning, the electric detonator wouldn't work! This potential disaster was averted by the quick thinking, experienced sapper Corporal. He promptly disconnected the detonator and wired the cable to the Spartan battery, touching the ends together at the right time, to create the necessary electric pulse to detonate the batsims; and delivering the artillery barrage on schedule. Bright blokes, these sappers.

Back in the base, life went on. Much of my job was spent running the troop, which became more challenging once my staff sergeant was posted.

There were some perks though. I took some of my troop and others from the Squadron adventure training in Sardinia, which was a pleasant change from icy Germany. The sappers were well behaved and rose to the challenge of some of the more interesting hike routes I had chosen across the island. In hindsight, some of the cliff top treks I led were decidedly dicey and I soon learnt that not every sapper has a head for heights. But they, we, all did it, overcoming fear, which is what adventure training is all about.

One evening in Sardinia, nearly back at our base, but leading the group through a seemingly deserted farm, I was ambushed by a rather large farm dog. The dog was of the Alsatian variety, with an apparent dislike for visitors. It came bounding towards me like a greyhound from the trap. I remembered that we have dominion over animals. I remembered that I should not show fear. And I remembered I had a party of sappers right behind me who would be very interested to see what I would do next.

I stood still, looked at the dog and held out my hand, saying 'Stop there in Jesus name.'

And it did. Then it trotted off back to its kennel.

The sappers joined me, looking surprised. One said 'Blimey Sir, Crocodile Dundee!'

That night, the incident triggered a lively conversation about my Christian faith, when after a beer, tongues loosened.

When I had first arrived in Germany, the Regimental Padre had introduced himself to me and on finding that I was a

Christian decided I could say something about my faith to the squadron at its next church parade. He did not seem to enjoy doing sermons. I accepted his offer, even though I was not completely happy with his motive, because I knew I might as well let people know where I stood. It seemed to go OK. I cannot remember what I said but, knowing me, it would probably have been sensible stuff about being inspired by men like King David and Joshua. It went down quite well, even if it raised some eyebrows. My soon-to-be-posted Staff Sergeant nodded to me from across his desk in the Troop Office the next day and said, 'More power to your elbow, Sir, well done for not hiding your light under a bushel!'

I knew I would now be watched, based on the squash court incident during my attachment to the UK engineer regiment the year before. Christians, please remember again that our walk with Christ in the workplace can be like living in the proverbial goldfish bowl; the world watches us to see that our walk with the Lord is genuine.

Having seen that I was not ashamed of my faith, of which I had never made any secret, following the Sardinian farmyard dog incident the guys were now curious. Rumours were starting to circulate in the squadron that we might go on an operational tour the next year and rightly, the sappers wanted to size up their officer. They simply wanted to know if they could rely upon an officer who was a member of the 'God-Squad' in a combat situation. Quite right, too.

It is potentially an awkward question, yet a very necessary one. All I could do was to describe my convictions about the legality in the eyes of the Lord of killing when necessary to do so, but not committing murder. After all, the Lord had given the command to Moses before telling Joshua to conquer the Promised Land.

That was fair enough, was the comment from the floor, but would I fire first? To which my simple reply was that I would, if it was to protect their lives, my life or the lives of people we were ordered to protect.

There were no further questions, the boys carried on drinking and I moved onto Cola; we went back to Germany soon after that.

Chapter 8 - Germany Life and Lifestyle

Hebrews 10:24-25:
'And let us consider how we may spur one another on towards love and good deeds, not giving up meeting together, as some are in the habit of doing, but encouraging one another and all the more as you see the ay approaching.'

I was missing Christian fellowship though. I am sure I was the only Christian in the squadron or, at least, the only one willing to admit it. There was a garrison church which attracted a small group of believers. There were a few wives and one of the teachers from the garrison English-speaking primary school for the soldiers' children. Not the full thriving UK churches I had grown used to and of course some differing theological views, too.

So, if I was on the base during a weekend, I would try to go along to the church to support it because it was the local expression of Christianity that my UK military community would understand. I resisted the temptation to try and find a local lively German church because I felt a strong obligation to not distance myself from the army. This was a tough call for me.

I had to deal with the sense of spiritual isolation and the only way to do that is to spend time with the Lord. I prayed a lot and read the Bible many times. I may not have understood parts of it, but we spend our lives in Christ obtaining revelation from His Word anyway.

I found Bible characters like Daniel really spoke to me because I felt I could partially identify with the sense of being exiled to a foreign land and culture, whilst knowing that the Lord was with me and that I had to stand up for Him. And I did (and still do) stand up for Him, despite the common mistakes I made. My desire to keep this book relatively concise and readable prevents me from listing all my mistakes!

Sappers all knew ways to find out more about their new Troop Commander. One such 'rite of passage' that was not everyone's cup of tea took place near the local river at a small Royal Engineers training site where basic watermanship skills were normally tested. The road crossed the river on one of those German 'bowstring' arch bridges of steel construction, with its steel supporting arches rising either side of the road to 30 feet above its surface; it looked similar to the Sydney Harbour Bridge. The wide metal girder 'bows', each of which braced the road bridge on either side of the carriageways, left the road surface at a reasonably steep curve which gradually lessened until you reached the apex of the bridge, about 60 feet above the river.

The 'rite of passage' was to run up to this apex of the bridge, without wobbling and landing on the road, and jump off into the river below.

Well, my new troop were very keen to see what their Troop Commander did next. I knew I had to take the bull by the horns and go for it, because weighing up the risk would appear indecisive and opting to not do it would severely dent my embryonic credibility.

So up I went, not looking down, in as steady a manner as I was able and reached the top. I did a smart left-hand turn and stared out across Western Germany. I was very aware of a pack of voyeuristic upturned faces looking in my direction and the river looked a long way away. I recalled Matthew 4, where Jesus was tempted by the devil to step off the highest point of the temple. But it was too late. Mouthing a silent 'Sorry Lord!' I stepped off into the void.

I remember thinking 'This falling is going on for a long time…' SPLASH as, a few seconds later, I finally hit the water. I had remembered to keep my legs together, eyes shut and everything crossed (not fingers though!) and bobbed back to the surface quickly. Relief. The sappers were satisfied in their nodding way; I didn't really know them yet. But they didn't know me and I knew the real test was to do it again, when you already knew what was involved and overcome fear of the known, not the unknown. They could claim ignorance had helped me if I left it at just one jump.

So up I went again, apologizing to the Lord that I was honestly not trying to put Him to the test. It was twice as frightening as before, but I was twice as determined to do it. Up to the top of the bowstring bridge I climbed again and threw myself off like a free-fall lemming. Same dull Splash, but a few more raised eyebrows from my watching Field Troop sappers; which was the effect I wanted. Word would get around in the tight community that was the engineer regiment in Germany.

The British Army culture in Germany was very social and often involved a lot of alcohol. I have mentioned that each squadron had its own bar in the attic space of its accommodation. I suspect there was a military common sense approach which viewed it as preferable to keep drunken sappers on the base, lurching a few yards back to their accommodation with an occasional fight, instead of going into the local town as a whooping group, mixing it and causing problems with the locals and police. Altercations with the local population were far harder to unravel than incidents on base, which were subject to military law and solvable by either the squadron OC or regimental CO. I remembered some of these stories from the year before.

Another 'rite of passage' took place in the squadron bar. This was the social hub for the squadron sappers. I was invited to meet my new Field Troop there socially, soon after I met them for the standard 'Meet the Troopy' ceremony, when they get to see what you are like when you have had a lot to drink. I paced myself, which irritated one or two of them, but otherwise I had a good evening and I reckon the Troop did, too. At the end of the night, a pint of Cola was passed to me and I was invited to down it in one. No problem – I had been quite good at that as a non-Christian so I raised the glass to my lips and drained away.

Just after the halfway point I realised that it did not taste quite like Cola and when I finished it, the sappers let out a great cheer. My drink had been spiked with every spirit available at the bar, whisky, vodka, brandy and so on; I had swallowed quite a Molotov Cocktail. I could feel it simmering in my guts like hot fat on a barbeque.

Thankfully everyone was going back to their accommodation, and so did I. I went straight to the toilet, knelt beside the porcelain and was very sick indeed. I think the correct term is that I had a long conversation on the big white telephone. I have never let that happen to me again.

In the regiment, the standard weekend, particularly for single people such as those living in the officers' mess, was to finish work by 5pm, grab a meal, do some fitness and then get on the beer. Saturday morning sleep off the effects of the night before, have a brunch, watch TV, do some admin, have a meal and then back on the beer. Sunday morning sleep it off the previous night for longer, have some lunch, do some admin in the afternoon ready for work again on the Monday.

I know I am simplifying things a bit and it was not all beer, beer, beer, but sometimes it felt like it. I found a few simple solutions to prevent myself from sliding into this lifestyle, without distancing myself from the very colleagues to whom I was trying to represent the life of Jesus Christ.

So, I offered to drive on a night out, and be the 'Duty Driver'. The deal was that I drove, but no one was to be sick in my car. Being 'Duty Driver' has its moments and I'd learned this at Sandhurst, where my record was squeezing eight fellow officer cadets into my Renault 11 after a party, which I would not now recommend. Going over speed bumps was a hair-raising experience. In Germany, the reputation of the Polizei was such that I would not take that risk. Plus, I had bought a new car, because a tax agreement allowed Germany based personnel to lawfully buy a new vehicle tax-free, so I was not about to have my shining new Peugeot 306 impounded. But it did mean that I could ferry us all to pubs (because officers were not supposed to frequent squadron bars too often; the boys needed their space) and my fellow officers were happy to go somewhere other than the officers' mess for the evening. And I was free to remain sober enough to drive.

I also tried to drink something other than Cola, because litres of sugar solution swallowed through an evening risked leaving me in a worse state than consuming the equivalent amount of German lager. So, I hit upon a mix of orange juice and coke, which in Germany is called spritze and in the UK, is known as 'Muddy Puddle'. Try it. It is surprisingly good. Though when back in the UK, in one snobby Surrey pub they asked me to drink it in the corner near the door in case their regular customers thought they were selling bad Guinness.

I drew on the wisdom of God though, to know how to walk out my faith as a professional officer. I believe there to be no short cut from reading the Bible and praying to the Lord and speaking in tongues, especially when fellowship is irregular.

All the time I was mindful of verses like the following in 1 John 2:15-17:

> 'Do not love the world or anything in the world. If anyone loves the world, love for the Father is not in them. For everything in the world – the lust of the flesh, the lust of the eyes, and the pride of life – comes not from the Father but from the world. The world and its desires pass away, but whoever does the will of God lives for ever.'

That spoke to me of a healthy distinction between my life in Christ and the lifestyle that many of my fellow officers were living. They were a good bunch, though, and I learned it is a short step from maintaining that healthy distinction to becoming 'holier than thou' in attitude. I kept remembering John 3:16:

> 'God so loved the world that He gave...'

I reckon every Christian must work that out for themselves. It is so easy if you are part of a busy church to only have Christian friends; it is so much easier and seemingly safer. But the great commission of Matthew 28:18-20 is very clear.

> 'Then Jesus came to them and said, 'All authority in heaven and on earth has been given to me. Therefore, go and make disciples of all nations, baptising them in the name of the Father and of the Son and of the Holy Spirit, and teaching them to obey everything I have commanded you. And surely, I am with you always, to the very end of the age.'

We are in the world, not of it and yet we are also the salt of the earth. The question for all of us is, who are we salting?

My fellow officers were generally good company. One or two certainly were openly unimpressed about my faith in Jesus and I took quite a bit of teasing. One of the subjects that came up was the fact that I was not pursuing successful amorous adventures with flighty young ladies as they all were (or said they were). I ignored the flickering concern of the accusations I had received at Sandhurst repeating themselves and decided that absolute honesty was the best policy.

I said that as a Christian, I believe in no sex outside of marriage, that I was a virgin and would remain so until I was married. And right now, I had not met the right one.

That provoked quite a stunned silence in the officers' mess bar. Some could not believe it and were quite rude, others were impressed but did not say, and still others said good luck to me but that was a path they had no intention of taking. Still, it cleared the air though! Alas, I did pick up a nick name; 'Bishop's-Parts', which could have been worse and was thankfully abbreviated to 'Bishop'. I would have preferred something relating more to Nehemiah, but you cannot have everything, I suppose.

Still, life could go on and there were lots of interesting opportunities outside of regimental life. Four of us piled into a car for Easter and drove to Prague for the bank holiday weekend. That was a great excursion. The route was a pleasant drive through Saxony, and we knew when we had reached the old East Germany by the deterioration in the roads. It was only a few years after the collapse of the Berlin Wall.

And the new Czech Republic was emerging as a very healthy nation. Prague was an absolute gem of a place, well before UK stag parties had it in their sights. The old town was unspoilt, the food & drink low priced and excellent, and it was a pleasure to spend time with three good friends in an historic old city. We even went to the opera! I said at the outset that I would not be exploring any brothels etc. and having made my gentle, but firm stand, funnily enough, they too were not keen to plunge into pagan revelry either. Not every person who does not have a Christian faith is a hedonistic heathen and there are many men and women of peace out there who are just ready and willing to chat. It was good to do so.

Mind you, one or two of my fellow officers were live wires. There was a pair of Troop Commanders in the other field squadron who were referred to as 'Denizens of Irresponsibility' by the Guard Commander for their refusal to take life too seriously. And their prank on the CO's dog was memorable. I was on leave and told about it, or I might have objected to it on grounds of animal welfare. But probably not; it was too funny.

The CO's dog often came into the officers' mess. It was a large, friendly, slobbering stud bull mastiff. It would bumble round the ante-room and bar area, hoovering up crisps and unattended sandwiches, leaving white ridges of saliva on the officers' mess furniture. Unfortunately, the saliva was not the only body product left behind by this dog and I will leave to your imagination what evidence there was of the visit of a stud bull mastiff in our home.

Now these two officers decided enough was enough and knew that it would be difficult to approach the CO on this matter. So, they hatched a simple plan to make the point. One day they fed the dog so that its front end was busy, whilst applying gentian violet stain to the dog's rather large testicles at the other end. The bull mastiff was oblivious to its glowing testimonials, but for a short season made quite a statement when in the public eye. The point was made and on returning from leave, I saw no evidence of visits to the officers' mess from the CO's dog.

Germany is such a pleasant country in which to live, being green, friendly and clean. I enjoyed getting away for trips of my own on the weekend, practicing my German, often when my brother officers were too hung over to want to do anything in the morning or afternoon. I took my Bible as well and just had time with the Lord, whilst exploring the area.

Fellowship was always a challenge, though, in Germany. I attended any OCU Germany events that I could, but also went to meet up with other Christian young officers like me in their British Army bases in Germany.

I remember visiting one Christian friend who was on one of the tank bases based near Soltau. He was having a hard time as the REME officer attached to a tank regiment. The tank regiment officers' mess was stereotypical cavalry officer and unlike most I visited, quite snobby. My friend, like me, had not gone to public school nor had the same background of his fellow officers and so felt quite ostracised by them. The base location, far out from the local towns, did not help the sense of isolation. It was good to see him though, to encourage each other in the Lord and pray together. In Christ, a burden shared is a burden reduced and well on the way to being dealt with.

I remember being told about a similar situation in a rather 'exclusive' officers' mess where the existing officers took against a new arrival, perhaps from a different social class. Apparently, his car was a different make to those of the other officers. Anyway, one night these officers all got together, probably after a beer or two, and decided to 'trash' the new officer's car because in their opinion it was not a car appropriate for an officer. Consequently, the car ended up being very badly damaged.

The CO of the regiment heard about this incident very soon afterwards and invited all the young officers responsible to come and explain what they had done and why. The CO was of a similar background to these officers and was leaning back in his chair, sitting behind his desk when his young officers (not including the new arrival of the trashed car) trooped into his office to explain.

When they had all assembled and closed the door behind, the CO smiled and leant forward in a conspiring manner. He asked what issue they had been hoping to address? Their spokesman, prompted by the group and reassured at the CO's evident empathy, explained to him that a car like the new arrival's was 'unofficerlike' and that they, as regimental officers, had chosen to do something about it. There was a murmur of assent from the rest of the group, with vigorous nods.

'Hmmm, I see,' nodded the CO, looking thoughtful as he leant back in his chair. 'And what is an appropriate car for a new arrival to our regiment to have?'

That was easy; the group reckoned on an equivalent of a brand-new Volkswagen Golf, similar to what most of them owned.

'Excellent!', said the CO, suddenly leaning forward and springing his premeditated trap, 'You can all club together and buy him a new one!'

And so, they did.

I must point out that while this may fit with a stereotypical view of ex-public school army officer's messes, my personal experience is that I have found every army officers' mess that I have lived in to be welcoming and hospitable, irrespective of the background of its officers.

Garrison life was busy but good. There was continual training to do, be it rifle shooting or fitness marches, or checking all the stores were still there. An endless task was the maintenance of the Field Troop Vehicles, which were made up of a Spartan and four 432s. This was a full-time job, because there are a lot of things that can go wrong on a tracked vehicle and an awful lot of things that can go wrong on elderly tracked vehicles. My vehicles were not young. Tracked vehicles need to be operating quite often to keep ticking over and we were struggling to do this, so vehicles were requiring a lot of maintenance.

I had a new Staff Sergeant now, who was a larger-than-life character. A very experienced combat engineer, who could plan a bridge with his eyes shut and knew all about sapper tracked vehicles. When he arrived, he knew just who to talk to (or threaten!) to get the Field Troop vehicles up and running. Which he did. His experience certainly triumphed over my youthful enthusiasm.

He was a straight-talking Yorkshireman and took his role of controlling the Field Troop seriously, whilst giving me good advice at raising my game to get better at commanding it. He taught me a lot about battle procedure, the importance of passing information early to my Field Troop, so that even if the information was incomplete, yet accurate, the Field Troop could get ahead with being ready for the next task. He loved his rugby and his rugby songs and became quite a rallying point for the new Squadron SNCOs as they were gradually posted in to bring the squadron back up to full strength.

I had a couple of good leave breaks that year and I made the most of them. I urge the reader to not fritter time off from work that you do get, especially leave or holiday. Life is always busy and we all have responsibilities, but I have found that marriage and children see those responsibilities increase, not lessen.

Back in the early nineties, I was young, free and single. I had the freedom to think only of myself. While singleness is not everyone's ideal state, especially that of a young Christian, it does have certain advantages. While even then, my desire was to find the right girl and get married, I knew that not having found her at that stage did enable me to have different opportunities. For me, it was the chance to travel at relatively short notice to some interesting locations. Having a disposable income as an army officer helped to fund this!

Therefore, if you are single and can travel, do it. This is because you don't know when you will have the chance to do so again. I know that most single Christians wish to be married and it is my strong belief that if a Christian has a desire to be married, then the Lord will act to make that happen. In the meantime, singleness brings opportunities that are harder to take when one is married. The Bible describes this in 1 Corinthians 7.

So, before I was married, I took the opportunity to visit many countries and I am glad I did so when I could; now I am married with children there are less opportunities because I have my family to think of now. But back then, young, free and single, I was becoming determined to make the most of any time off I received as an officer and so a leave period was an ideal slot in which to broaden my horizons.

For the first break I had an enjoyable, solo trip to Poland via the former East Germany; I was unable to persuade my fellow officers to accompany me on a train trip into deepest Poland.

I visited Wittenberg, where Martin Luther posted his '95 Theses' on the church door in 1517, which heralded the Protestant Reformation. On into Poland, and visited Poznan, Wroclaw, Warsaw and then south to Krakow. The Polish cities were great, but Krakow really is superb. I daresay much has changed since I was there. Like Prague, it is now on the stag party agenda and that does not help a town's reputation. The Poles were charming, more so when they found out I was not German, but British and in the army as well and I spent a very pleasant few days there.

Of course, this was around the time that 'Schindler's List' was screened, the events of which took place and were subsequently filmed in Krakow. Quite sobering then, to visit the Jewish Quarter where once 250,000 Jews lived before the war, to find only 250 living there. I trust the numbers have increased somewhat since then. I also felt I should go to Auschwitz, which is hardly an enjoyable day out, but a very necessary one. I had not appreciated the scale of the operation run by the Nazis, or how well organised it was, nor how much of the German war effort was used in the final solution. But the grim tragedy is seeing the huge numbers of people, whose only crime was to be different to the Nazi ideal, who suffered such an undeserved and miserable fate in Auschwitz.

Suitably educated, back to Germany I went.

The second leave period involved a trip to Virginia Beach, USA to participate in the Association of Military Christian Fellowships' conference. I went with a good friend and fellow officer in the Lord, who was also a strong a OCU member, and I flew out to New York, hired a car (I was now the right age) and drove south.

The USA is such a pleasure to visit. American people are friendly, talkative and there is a lot to see. We visited the

Amish communities and had a good look round the Battlefield of Gettysburg, scene of Pickett's Charge and 'the High-Water Mark of the Confederacy'. The conference itself was interesting, seeking to establish common ground in Christ across the different military Christian fellowships of the world. At that time, Christian fellowships were starting to emerge from the former Eastern Bloc countries, most notably Poland, but others too, so it was an exciting time to network. Encouraging others, particularly officers, to grow their passion to stand for Jesus in the military environment became quite a passion of mine later in my army career.

We returned to New York afterwards, and saw the sights. We climbed the twin towers before anyone had even heard of Osama Bin Laden. We also visited some great restaurants, the most entertaining of which was a Jewish one, where my pal inadvertently asked for a bacon sandwich. He received a bleak look from the waiter. Appalled at his mistake, he tried again, and inadvertently asked for a prawn cocktail. The waiter's look was now even bleaker. In hindsight, we would have done well to have studied Leviticus 11 before our visit. We left and dined elsewhere.

Back in Germany, the rumour was that we were getting a new OC and that in the summer, we would be deployed to Bosnia on 'Operation Grapple'. This UK military operation was very much ongoing as the UN continued to wrestle with the Yugoslavian conundrum. This coincided with me getting the timings wrong for medicals for the squadron boxing team, which meant half of them were ineligible for the regimental boxing competition. Consequently, I picked up a lot of extra orderly officer duties over Christmas. Still, the Regimental Adjutant was a decent man and he accepted that I may not be able to get home at Christmas, but could line up my duties so that I could go skiing with the OCU for the Christmas break instead.

At this time, the squadron was informed that early in the New Year it would get its new OC and that we could expect to deploy to Bosnia in March. Quite a pre-Christmas bombshell, which meant the New Year would be a busy one.

Ironically, I quite enjoyed being on duty for the first phase of the festive period. The regiment was quiet, being on 'stand down' for nearly three weeks. I had time to read up on the situation in Bosnia and get my mind onto what would probably be a very lively next year.

I was invited to visit many of the married officer's homes over Christmas and for New Year's Eve whilst on duty, I went over to the Technical Quartermaster's home for the evening. He had a ferocious reputation, and a German wife who was no shrinking violet, but we got on rather well. As a late entry officer, he had been Regimental Sergeant Major of another regiment before and I heard many tales of the grip he had on his unit. One that still lingers in my memory is that for a week prior to the Remembrance Sunday parade on his parade square, he had sent sappers into the trees to pull off all the remaining leaves. This was so that on the day of the parade, no unsightly leaves would drift across the open space to mar the event.

The squadron SNCOs were less charitable about him and one of them said of him:

"If the world were awash with urine, and he were in the only tree, I'd tread water."

In an army full of tough RSMs, he had acquired the impressive nickname of 'The Beast'. I rather liked him – he was intelligent and experienced, and the fact I spoke passable German and had explored the area cut some ice with him. But no-one messed with him and he knew it. On New Year's Eve, I told the Guard Commander that I was at the Technical Quartermaster's home for the evening. He took a breath and mindful of 'The Beast' and his ferocious reputation, murmured 'Good luck then, Sir!'

When I reached his house, 'The Beast' rang the guardroom to say that if there was a problem to ring his home. That meant I could relax. What I later found out was that he had taken the phone off the hook! If there had been an emergency the Guardroom Land Rover would have been sent round soon enough, but I had a great, interruption free evening. Thank you to a great Technical Quartermaster and his wife!

The OCU skiing week was a such an uplifting time of fellowship and made a significant difference to my subsequent tour in Bosnia. It is always good to be with God's people, especially if you have been in exile. My pal with whom I had visited the USA was there, plus a good crowd of other Christian officers. We were skiing in Austria and I loved driving down there and back from my base in Germany. Skiing is such a great sport with a bunch of fun, 'yeehaaing' fellow Christians, healthy and stimulating, with lots of adrenaline, aching legs and laughter.

More important than all of that, though, was the practical Biblical encouragement I received from a well-respected senior female officer of the British Army, who now does outstanding international ministry work. She and the speaker, who was an American senior officer were (and are) full of the Lord and His word and they showed me for the first time how to take hold of Scriptures for yourself and claim them to overcome challenges.

My challenge was that I was quite intimidated about deploying to Bosnia.

Now I know it would probably not measure up in danger level to anything that British Army units have since faced in Iraq and Afghanistan after the war on terror began. But this was before that, and at that time all Yugoslavia looked like from the outside was a seething cauldron of hatred, with Serbs, Croats and Bosnians cutting lumps out of each other and the UN peacekeepers being caught in the cross fire. And I was leading troops into that. But please bear with me if you are an Iraq or Afghanistan veteran.

I wanted to represent Jesus well, lead my soldiers well and not let anyone down. While the Lord had been so faithful to me that year, I had not found everything easy and I wanted to live in a fuller assurance of the Lord's hand on my life than ever before.

The scripture the two officers gave me was Psalm 91. As they showed me how to meditate on it and its truth (and I don't mean Yoga, I mean simply thinking about the Scripture and not any fears I might have), it steadily changed my anxiety into excitement. I am happy to quote Psalm 91 in full below:

1   *Whoever dwells in the shelter of the Most High will rest in the shadow of the Almighty.*
2   *I will say of the Lord, 'He is my refuge and my fortress, my God, in whom I trust.'*
3   *Surely he will save you from the fowler's snare and from the deadly pestilence.*
4   *He will cover you with his feathers, and under his wings you will find refuge; his faithfulness will be your shield and rampart.*
5   *You will not fear the terror of night, nor the arrow that flies by day,*
6   *nor the pestilence that stalks in the darkness, nor the plague that destroys at midday.*
7   *A thousand may fall at your side, ten thousand at your right hand, but it will not come near you.*
8   *You will only observe with your eyes and see the punishment of the wicked.*

>9 If you say, 'The Lord is my refuge,' and you make the Most High your dwelling,
>10 no harm will overtake you, no disaster will come near your tent.
>11 For he will command his angels concerning you to guard you in all your ways;
>12 They will lift you up in their hands, so that you will not strike your foot against a stone.
>13 You will tread on the lion and the cobra; you will trample the great lion and the serpent.
>14 'Because he loves me,' says the Lord, 'I will rescue him; I will protect him, for he acknowledges my name.
>15 He will call on me, and I will answer him; I will be with him in trouble, I will deliver him and honour him.
>16 With long life I will satisfy him and show him my salvation.'

I returned for duty in Germany encouraged, inspired and ready to take on the challenges that lay ahead. The year had been a challenging one for me, where I had not found Troop Commanding easy when I did not have the expected Staff Sergeant to assist me for quite a period of it and to not have much of a Troop in terms of numbers, either. Yes, I had enjoyed some great experiences, but taking your Field Troop on deployment to a combat zone is where the rubber hits the road and it becomes very real. Mistakes can have horrendous consequences and success must be properly handled.

Which is why Psalm 91 was such a bedrock to me, because it was more than just sentimental comfort; it was the Word of the Lord and I was willing and able to trust it and Him.

I cannot describe what a change it was for me to begin to learn how to take hold of the Word of the Lord for myself. Shortly after receiving Psalm 91 as an encouragement, the Lord gave me a few lines of verse which enabled me to crystallise what my salvation had meant to me and so I could begin to articulate what it could mean to other people.

On a few scraps of paper, I scribbled down this poem, whilst on the OCU ski party where the Lord blessed me so much. Now, it seems a little religious and 'clunky', but it does show where I was at pre-Bosnia and so I judge it right to include it. With some light subsequent editing by me, here it is below:

Salvation
Part One: Old Testament

We have a promise centuries old,
The greatest story ever told,
Of God's great plan to deal with sin,
And allow mankind to dwell with Him.

When Eve ignored and ate the fruit,
House-trained Adam followed suit,
A rebellion that our Lord won't pardon,
So mankind was banished from the garden.

A paradox has taken place,
God from our sins must turn His face,
But still He wants us all to be,
In Heaven with Him for eternity.

So desperate measures must now be taken,
Man must from his sin be shaken,
For we constant sinners don't pass inspection,
For we fail to meet our Lord's perfection.

Israel rejected the prophets God sent,
Despite the exile, and failed to repent,

And stiff-necked remained the Jewish nation,
Unable to receive God's salvation.

The prophets had failed, they'd been ignored;
Mankind still far from peace with the Lord,
But all is not lost, the best is to come,
God, in His mercy, will send us His Son.

Part 2: New Testament

Jesus was born, a man like us, grew up in Palestine, Galilee,
Suffered trials, temptations, hurt and pain, but obeyed God perfectly.

The only man to live the life, to fulfil God's law to the letter,
The only man to deserve salvation, for no other man followed God better.

But the chasm remains 'twixt God and man, only perfection can bridge the gap,
Perfection personified in Christ the Lord, can lead us across without mishap.

Our imperfection we cannot solve, God's known that since the fall,
But worthy is God's only Son, to carry sin for us all.

So we believe in a Holy God, who loved us when all our efforts failed,
So much He'd let His own son suffer, and to a cross be cruelly nailed.

Sin is death, the Bible says, sin frequents the devil's domain,
But Jesus' cross conquered Satan's works, when Jesus died and rose again.

Jesus has blazed the trail for us, He's paid the price, the road is clear,
To Heaven, when we submit to Him, when we face the world and persevere.

So the story has not ended yet, Jesus the Judge will soon be sent,
To claim His flock who know His voice, and reject those who did not repent.

If you've repented, you have crossed the gap, Christ receives you whatever your state,
If not then you have still got time, to approach the cross before it's too late.

OCU Ski Party
Austria
The nineties!

Back to work in the New Year, the first squadron parade after the Christmas break was the inevitable Battle Fitness Test of a three-mile timed run to make sure no-one had gone to seed over the leave period. Our new OC had just arrived and the build up to the squadron and my Field Troop's deployment on Operation Grapple to Bosnia was about to begin.

Chapter 9 - Pre-Bosnia, the Warm Up

Proverbs 23:12:

'Apply your heart to understanding and your ears to words of knowledge.'

Proverbs 27:23:

'Be sure you know the condition of your flocks, give careful attention to your herds.'

The new OC was an experienced sapper officer who had a good reputation as a leader and had done well in staff jobs, such as Divisional Adjutant and on the various army staff college courses. He had less than three months before deploying on Operation Grapple with his field squadron and the churn of personnel in and out of the squadron had not helped it form fully as a unit. My 'new' Staff Sergeant was posted on, to the Royal School of Military Engineering to be another QMSI. This was promotion for him, but he was very disappointed to not be going to Bosnia.

I now had my third Troop Staff Sergeant in a twelve-month period.

It is time for me to explain a little more to non-military readers about a Royal Engineers Troop Staff Sergeant. They are often known as the Troop 'Staffy', a term which I use occasionally throughout this book. I invariably addressed him as 'Staff', sometimes followed by his surname.

When I served as a Royal Engineers Troop Commander, the relationship with your Troop Staff Sergeant (the 'Staffy') had a major impact on the officer's success or otherwise. This relationship is worth a book in its own right, but when I was a very junior officer, it was explained to me that the Troop Commander commanded, while the Troop Staffy controlled, the Royal Engineer Field Troop. This meant I gave the orders and the Staffy ensured that they were properly obeyed.

My new Troop Staff Sergeant, 'Staff' Smith, was a superb Royal Engineer who was loyal, tough, humorous and professional. A thick set, solidly built ex-paratrooper, he took his role as Troop Commander's mentor very seriously and I learnt a lot about management and leadership from him. Good Field Troop Staff Sergeants often ensured that the Troop Commander's orders were sensible by checking them first for any gaffs, and then ensured that the Corporals and sappers obeyed them in the spirit in which they were given; I had an excellent one in Staff Smith.

As other chapters show, when I first turned up at the regiment, a year or so before deploying to Bosnia, it had not been a settled time and I certainly would have liked to have flourished. Some of it like the boxing medicals had been my own fault, but a lot of it was not. I had not had a Troop Staff Sergeant for a few months and had not found it easy without this experienced SNCO mentor that most young officers need (if they are honest) to make a success of their first command. Staff Smith became my Troop Staff Sergeant a few weeks before Bosnia, came from within the regiment, and so thankfully we were not strangers.

Staff Smith had observed me bearing up under some unjust circumstances (as 1 Peter urges us to do) and had decided that

I was a better officer than I thought I was. This is an important point, because many times we allow our own negative view of ourselves to dictate what we think about who we are. The Bible says 'as a man thinks, so he is', and so a negative view of yourself is projected outwards and affects how we come across as a leader and as a human being. If this negativity is not stopped a vicious downwards spiral develops and a Christian must not allow these lies to rule him or her. We are 'fearfully and wonderfully made' and 'the head and not the tail' and 'seated in heavenly places in Christ'. And we need to believe this or we are believing the devil's lies. Personally, I would rather believe the trustworthy message that Jesus tells us through His Word. I am always impressed at how confident Nehemiah is in his sense of calling, mission and purpose.

It has taken me many years to grasp this. Back then, the Lord was gracious to me, as always, and Staff Smith was a great encouragement to me; he saw my potential as a leader and enjoyed coaching a willing workhorse like me. I wanted to be the best and I am not ashamed of that at all. I still do and so should every Christian; Jesus has invested himself in each of us and He deserves the best, too.

So, when Staff Smith first arrived at my Field Troop, he was candid enough to say that I had all the makings of a sound officer, but was frank enough to say that I still had a lot to learn. And my goodness, did I have a lot still to learn.

He found my Christian faith amusing at first, though I believe he respected me for it because I was reasonably consistent in lining up my lifestyle, with my beliefs, with my confession of faith. I also took his advice seriously, because he was a very experienced soldier, who had served on many operational tours before and applied his experience with wisdom. We got on very well.

It was just as well we did.

The new OC proved to be quite a force to be reckoned with and he was very clear that the squadron was not where he wanted it to be if it were to deploy imminently on Operation Grapple. We had a new Squadron Second-in-Command, or 2i/c, as it is known, to manage squadron staffing and a new Squadron Operations Officer (Ops Officer) to organise training. This left Troop Commanders and their Staff Sergeants to sort out their respective Field Troops. There was a new Squadron Quartermaster and new Staff Sergeants running the squadron transport, stores and signals on his behalf. The Squadron Sergeant Major remained, and that was good. I grew to like and respect him more and more as the build-up developed, and on into the deployment itself. A new Troop Commander arrived, and he and I became good friends. He, the other Troop Commander and I worked well together.

The OC was very driven, and he was quite right to be. He wanted to form a sound squadron team quickly and he did so through determined, ruthless usage of the chain of command (or management structure). That meant that he expected the Field Troop Commanders to command their troops and see that his instructions were obeyed. He did not want the Staff Sergeants to unwittingly usurp this, nor did he as OC want to micro-manage his Troop Commanders. This firm approach put me and my fellow 'Troopys' on our mettle from day one and was just what we needed. The sometimes piecemeal method of operating in a below-strength field squadron was rapidly dwindling into the past as the squadron reached its manning establishment.

This absence of micro-management is worth recording, because it demonstrated and taught me a style of leadership that I still apply today. Its official name is 'Mission Command' and it simply means giving a leader a task, with resources, a timing and any relevant constraints and then trusting them to get on with it.

It requires the leader trusting his or her subordinates and the subordinates being sufficiently empowered to make the task happen. It does not prevent review or clarification or change of the task. But it does facilitate initiative and enables the subordinate to work out their own way of doing it without every step being prescribed by the leader.

I suspect most people perceive the army to be a micro-manager's paradise, and while there were (and probably still are!) micro-managers in the army, often a subordinate is given considerable latitude by their commander to just complete the task. Personally, micro-managing people (as a leader and manager occasionally must do) is very time consuming and hinders a leader's strategic thinking. I much prefer Mission Command today, as I did back then.

I found it increasingly empowering being led and managed like this. It made me think things through, made me feel trusted and meant that I led and managed my Field Troop, especially my Corporal Section Commanders, in that way.

The fish rots from the head down and that is such a truism for organisations. How a leader operates is always reflected, at least in part, in the organisation they lead. A sloppy, unplanned leader will generally lead a sloppy, unplanned organisation. A firm, well organised and professional leader will lead a well-established, well organised and professional organisation. I saw this happening before my very eyes in the way this new OC got hold of his new squadron. I will resist the temptation to name him because I believe he is a senior sapper officer now and needs no testimony from me. He was not always popular, but I think he respected me, and I certainly respected him. He was a first-class OC.

And so, we trained for Bosnia. Most of the sappers went off for at least a week's refresher training in the Royal School of Military Engineering in the UK for their respective 'trades', so that the latent brick laying; painting; electrical; carpentry and other skills in a field troop were up to speed before deployment. We still had no clear idea of likely tasks.

We Troop Commanders revised our recce skills and how to build equipment bridges. We revised checking routes, planning construction tasks and field fortifications, as well as some of the background to the conflict. We taught our troops the Serbo-Croat phrases they would need, like 'Don't shoot I'm British!', or 'Stop or I shoot!', which all became cheery, beery standard greetings in the squadron bar; I suppose it shows at least the sappers learnt them.

The orders for opening fire were important, too, and it is an officer's job to be on top of these so that his soldiers are. We were going as peacekeepers wearing the blue UN headgear and vehicles painted white with UN livery. We were not deploying to Bosnia as war fighters, yet we had to be prepared to defend ourselves if any of the warring factions (Serb, Croat or Bosnian) wanted to pick a fight with us, or better still deter them from doing it in the first place. Deterrence was primarily achieved by looking, acting and being professional all the time, so that a warring faction would look elsewhere for a fight. Defence meant understanding the situation and boiled down to not firing the first shot unless it was clear that some enemy was about to have a go at us first. And if we were fired upon, our response was to be proportionate, not heavy handed, for fear of exacerbating an already tense situation which had so far caused many civilian casualties and was shredding a former European nation. So, explaining this so that it was known *and* understood took time, but it was worth it because it set the tone for what we were going to do.

The OC took time to get to know us, with dinner at his house and taking the time to impart what he expected of us and our

Field Troops. Communicating his vision is probably the modern term; we just enjoyed drinking his wine and learning a little more about what to expect!

We all went on mines awareness training because Bosnia was rapidly emerging as a place being covered with unmarked landmines because of the ongoing civil war. The consensus was to mark and avoid where possible and only walk on tarmac.

The different commanders within the squadron, which meant the officers, SNCOs and some of the JNCOs, deployed to Sennelager, another German training area like Soltau, where we met the army brigade we were to support. They were mainly infantry, from what was known as the County Regiments; these are battalions with long fighting traditions made up of very professional soldiers and officers. It was a good time to revise our weapons training skills, so we could all use our rifles properly, our GPMGs and in the officers' case, the pistol. I loved it. Weapons training is such fun and the days spent on Sennelager ranges were really valuable. The infantry does this sort of firepower stuff much more often than the sappers (because the infantry don't have to build bridges, waterpoints etc.) and they were good instructors.

We were shown the infantry AFV, the Warrior, a superb tracked Armoured Personnel Carrier with a 30mm Rarden cannon with a long range. This was demonstrated with the pulverising of some old car hulks at the far end of the range. It was good to know that several of these Warriors would be available as a Quick Reaction Force at our beck and call, should any of the warring factions want to start a fight with us using heavier weapons than those with which we were issued.

I remember one Lance Corporal instructor addressing the hundreds of us from the brigade as we stood on a low ridge in the Sennelager ranges. He had been tasked to reiterate how important accurate fire control orders were so that if there was a scrap, the Warrior AFVs could have their fire directed effectively and quickly, thus winning the firefight. Noticing the Brigadier standing in the crowd, the Lance Corporal, clearly from a rural part of the UK said:

'Excuse me Brigade Commaaahnderr, Zur, could you give uz a foire control orrderr as if there wuz enemy in they trees at the end of that there range?'.

The entire brigade caught its breath at the Lance Corporal's effrontery in making such a request for a fire control order, from such a senior officer as the Brigadier.

The Brigadier did not bat an eyelid, but stepped forward and gave an effortless, perfect, loud fire control order. Everyone nodded approvingly. Back came the Lance Corporal's reply:

'That wuz ex-err-lent, Zur, Oi wud reccermend yur promotion fur that wun!'

At which the rest of the Brigade let out a great shout of laughter at the bare-faced cheek of the man. I don't know if he was demoted to Private by the end of the day, or whether he remained a Lance Corporal for the rest of his career. Probably neither, for the British Army is surprisingly tolerant of jests like that.

My Field Troop and I had a demolitions training afternoon to conclude the training. We never knew whether we would need to rig explosives or not in Bosnia, so it did no harm to revise our skills. There was a demolitions training range in Sennelager, which was a reasonably remote patch of land and we refreshed the setting up of the different charges. Time constraints meant we had to blow them all up at the end of the afternoon and not stage by stage, as would have happened if we had been there all day.

Come the time of the great detonation, all the charges had been lined up, yet kept a distance apart so that one explosion does not disrupt and prevent the next one. It was good practice to stagger the detonations, so that the explosions could be counted from the bunker behind which the Field Troop sheltered. That way, by matching the number of explosions to the number of charges, we knew all the explosives had safely blown up and that none was left simmering to blow up later. Leaving an unexploded charge on the range was a huge no-no, because of its risk to subsequent range users.

Well, we set twenty charges and walked back to the bunker (you never run), took cover and initiated the explosions. Real life adventure stuff – actually being paid to blow things up!

But after explosion number nineteen there was a long silence. Staff Smith glanced across at me looking less relaxed than usual.

'Dunno about you, Sir,' he muttered 'but I only made that nineteen!'

I too had made it nineteen. A degree of fidgeting from the rest of the highly numerate Field Troop confirmed that they had counted nineteen, too. One charge had not gone off.

There are times when the buck stops with the leader and this was that time. I immediately stood up, ordered everybody to remain in cover, and asked for another charge to be made up. I knew that the procedure now was that someone had to walk out, lay another charge beside the one that had not yet exploded and detonate it so that both went up, thus removing the problem. And as the Troop Commander, the responsible officer and leader of the Field Troop, I knew that 'someone' was me.

I was passed the explosive charge by one of my reliable combat engineers, who very professionally kept a straight face and muttered in his deep Lancastrian accent 'Thur y'are, Sir, ohva t'you!'

And off I strode into the wasteland, praying earnestly in tongues as I did so.

I must admit my heart was thumping – the charge could go off at any time and unlike the Challenger tanks of a year ago, it would make quite a mess of me if it did. I looked for the charge amongst the wreckage caused by the other explosions and found it at last. It was one of the last charges and despite our efforts the detonator had been disrupted by one of the previous explosions. Well, I was not going to spend time diagnosing it! I placed the charge I was carrying beside it, initiated it and walked back to the bunker, now aware of one or two little faces peeping out from behind its shelter to hopefully see their Troop Commander being vaporised.

I reached the bunker in as calm a way as possible and sat down with as much studied nonchalance as I could muster. Thirty seconds later there was a colossal 'boom' as both charges went up and I exhaled gently.

The Lord looks after His own.

A few days later, Staff Smith drew me aside and quietly mentioned that he had been very impressed with the way I had handled the crisis by taking immediate responsibility and keeping the rest of the guys away. Of course, it was the Lord who had done it for me and kept me calm, but it did not seem right to say that. But the incident really helped develop our working relationship and I can only boast 'in the Lord' about it. After all, He stopped me from becoming vaporised.

Steadily, under its new OC, the squadron was coming together into a robust, resilient unit in time for its deployment. It was a madly busy time though and we worked many late evenings and weekends to get ready. I remember Staff Smith saying to me that we had to prioritise things to do, starting with whatever would trigger the biggest 'interview-without-coffee' if we didn't do it and then work back from there!

Looking back, it was a bit like the Valley of Dry Bones in Ezekiel 37 as the squadron came to life. We were finding out more about our likely tasks and location. So, the OC changed our orbat into two Field Troops and one large Support Troop. There were to be more route maintenance and plant tasks than we first thought, which is why Support Troop was enlarged and given an officer to command it. My other fellow Troop Commander and friend was to be detached with a smaller Field Troop, together with the Ops Officer, to another part of Bosnia to provide engineering support for a smaller British Army formation. And your correspondent was tasked to lead a slightly larger Field Troop at the squadron base in upcountry Bosnia, near to where the Brigade was located in order to be best placed to support it. Support Troop were also based with the squadron.

My Field Troop was in good shape like the squadron, with the Corporals I had received being good sappers. They liked Mission Command, too, and were as keen to prove their worth to their boss as I was keen to prove my worth to mine. They had a great sense of humour and, greatly encouraged by Staff Smith and I, took an almost paternal care of their (our!) sappers. My Troop Staff Sergeant knew far more about this than I did at the time, but just taking an interest in the people you lead can make such a difference to their well-being, manner and ability on the job. It is the same in the home, the church and any workplace.

One of the watch words I had decided upon for my Field Troop was that every piece of work we did, we would be proud to leave our name on and not skulk away hoping no-one noticed. I wonder how many of them remember that now?

The active encouragement, framed by Psalm 91, that I had received whilst skiing with the OCU was a stepping stone to a whole new place of confidence in the Lord and who He was calling me to be. I found a strength in the Lord that I had not previously enjoyed and it made a difference in my bearing and manner for that forthcoming year. That, and having a solid deputy in my Staff Sergeant meant that the Field Troop became more quietly confident as a body of men and smilingly ready for the challenges to come. I believe my growing spiritual wellness was reflected on the unit I was leading.

Standing on the Word of the Lord is both an easy thing to do, and an easy thing not to do; the difference is simple choice. I will admit to this being a lesson I have come back to more than I would care to admit, but I do know that the Lord guarantees His Word because He wrote it. It may not come to pass the way we expect, but the Lord does honour His word and it does not return to him void.

Most of the single guys took advantage of a weekend pass back to the UK to visit family and so did I. It was good to see my parents again and my Dad was naturally keen to hear what I would be doing. My Mum was a little circumspect about it and in my youthful naïve thinking I did not understand why; I was looking forward to the adventure. Now I am a parent, I have some idea of concern for my children's activities and I had under-estimated the implications to her of waving me off to a combat zone that was regularly in the news at the time.

And then it was time to deploy. The kit was packed, I locked my room in the Officers' Mess, waved goodbye to my Peugeot 306 in the Officers' Mess car park and stepped onto one of the waiting army buses along with the rest of my Field Troop and the squadron.

We were off to Bosnia!

Chapter 10 - Deployed to Bosnia

Nehemiah 4:17-18:
'Those who carried materials did their work with one hand and held a weapon in the other, and each of the builders wore his sword at his side as he worked.'

We landed in Split, Croatia and embussed into coaches that were waiting for us as arranged by the UN. We would be taking over vehicles and equipment from the Royal Engineer Field Squadron that we were relieving in central Bosnia and so it was just ourselves we were transporting. Most of our kit had been sent to the base in containers, so we travelled light, in uniform, with weapons, with our overnight kit.

The journey was memorable and I had not been on a coach trip like this before. The coach itself still had bullet holes in it from a previous encounter, through the windscreen mainly, but you could still see out. That quietened things down with the boys; not much singing on the bus at that point.

We set off up country through Croatia, then on into Bosnia proper via Mostar. Mostar was a shock. It was a city in the Former Republic of Yugoslavia in which the Croat and Bosnian Muslim minorities had co-existed peacefully for centuries. The outbreak of civil war in the region had set that co-existence ablaze, with the Croats on one side of the river shelling the Muslims on the other. This led to the destruction of the ancient 'Stari Most' or 'Old Bridge' over the river, which had traditionally joined the communities. Its demolition by shell fire became an iconic incident of the turmoil in what became known as the Former Republic of Yugoslavia or FRY.

Yugoslavia had emerged from the Second World War as a tightly run semi-dictatorship under a communist ex-partisan leader called Tito. He was a very autocratic, firm president and held Yugoslavia together; there was a concrete statue from those times that was still intact on one of the hills near our eventual base, a simple lump that the locals called 'Tito's Fist'. Yugoslavia needed a strong pair of hands. When Tito died, there was no successor and so the component republics began to break away. It is a long and complicated story, but in essence, the centre of Yugoslavia was a hotchpotch of different communities, whose boundaries overlapped between the modern-day countries of Serbia, Croatia and Bosnia.

Serbia wanted to protect ethnic Bosnian Serbs who lived in Bosnia. Croatians wanted to protect Bosnian Croats who also lived in Bosnia. The Bosnian Muslims, who were apparently Serbs who converted to Islam when the Ottomans invaded centuries before, felt threatened by this intrusion. The Serbs, who culturally were Orthodox Christians, detested the 'turn-coat' Bosnian Muslims for making this choice to embrace Islam. The traditionally Catholic Croats, who seemed to get on slightly better with the Bosnian Muslims, also felt threatened.

And so, it all got very nasty and it was in the FRY that the term 'ethnic cleansing' was coined. This meant the wiping out of entire groups of people based on their ethnicity. I won't describe what happened because it is not a pleasant tale, but central Bosnia was strewn with deserted houses, villages and towns where all that was left of a once thriving community were empty streets, lined with fire blackened houses and personal belongings scattered on the ground. The lucky ones were those that were given an hour or so's notice to pack and go. The unlucky ones were murdered in their own homes, which were then demolished about their bodies.

Eventually, as the fighting between these ethnic groups led to reprisals, and counter-reprisals, and then counter-counter-reprisals and so on, the Croats and Bosnian Muslims began to ease off on fighting each other because Serbia was growing as a perceived threat to them both. So, Bosnia and Croatia formed an uneasy alliance against Serbia, which backed the Bosnian Serbs, and so a rough line of battle was formed dividing the whole FRY. This was called the confrontation line and it moved quite a lot. Meanwhile, trouble continued because despite the alliance, various communities continued to exact revenge on each other for previous atrocities, and similar vendettas continued to be pursued between individuals. There were the awful atrocities of Zepa and Sebrinica, where the western Serbs were alleged to have massacred a lot of Bosnians.

At the time, all of us squadron officers wondered whether the defeat of the Bosnian Serbs would mean the Bosnian Muslims and Croats would turn on each other again. At the time, it was a fair question, but nowadays it does appear that life has settled down in the past two decades and that something akin to peace is fast returning to Bosnia under the Dayton Accord.

The UN deployed to Bosnia to 'keep the peace' but was largely toothless. However, it is easy to criticise, and the UN's presence was better than nothing at all. As a peacekeeper the UN did seem to operate with a different pace to the military one with which I was familiar. This remained frustrating. However, the UN provided a framework for something akin to normality to return to Bosnia, despite the inevitable tensions across Bosnia and within the UN nations present. The French, who were based in Sarajevo, the Bosnian capital, had quite a busy time of it, though the cynics claimed that that was because

French construction companies had won the city's rebuilding contracts!

It is all very well for me to say this, because as a busy Royal Engineers Field Troop Commander, I hardly had leisure time to over-familiarise myself with every strategic implication of Bosnia in the nineties. But I did know that we had a job to do and like the rest of my unit, wanted to get to our base and get on with it.

The squadron was located in the outskirts of a town right in the middle of this former Bosnian Muslim and Bosnian Croat conflict zone. Less than twelve months before, both communities had been trying to exterminate each other. The large valley in which the town itself lay was a sprawl of these gutted, blackened homes of once normal people who had experienced ethnic cleansing. The way to tell whether you were driving through a former Croat or Bosnian Muslim area was to see if there was a desecrated catholic church or mosque in the centre of the gutted houses. We never got out and 'rummaged' through those once happy dwellings, because for one thing it was disrespectful. Also, and even more importantly, our healthy awareness of the plethora of mines and booby traps likely to be there meant it was simply not worth the risk to life and limb. The estimate was that there were over 9000 unmarked mines in the town area alone. I was not going hill walking in the evenings, that was for sure.

I do remember being very grateful to the Lord that I had not had to grow up in a place where this kind of civil war had happened. Civil war does not benefit many and it certainly produces a lot of victims. I later saw pre-war pictures of the area when it was Yugoslavia, and it was a beautiful, prosperous, rural country with wooded hills and mountains. The stunning mountain scenery was still there when I arrived, but certainly not the prosperity. The town was smashed.

People still went around in traditional clothing, with the old men still wearing the Ottoman Fez as they sat drinking coffee in the shells of the once gaudy cafés. Farmers trying to get their livelihoods going again were using horses and carts. The women had hard faces and looked like they had suffered, too.

The base where the squadron was located was a large former warehouse complex outside the main town. We shared with an Infantry Company from one of the Scottish infantry regiments, who had the Warrior AFVs that we had seen demonstrated back in Germany. They were a tough lot and definitely the crew you'd want to call for fire support if needed. Mind you, they were not shy of the imposition of field discipline by their SNCOs on the private soldiers who dared to transgress. Even our outspoken OC reckoned we had enough to do without interfering:

'Leave those wee 'Leaping McNasties' to get on with it,' he advised.

We did.

We lived in 'Corrimec' portacabins, with one for every four sappers. Officers and SNCOs were allowed two to a 'Corrimec' and I shared with the Support Troop Commander; rank does have its privileges!

Also, sharing the base with us was a squadron of cavalry using Scimitar AFVs, which were like my old friend the Spartan. There was a sizeable REME presence, because there was a lot of military kit to service and we had a small British Army medical unit based on site, just in case.

The other half of the former warehouse complex was run by the UN, with whom we developed a strained relationship throughout the tour. We had turned up keen to get on with building things and they did not share our sense of urgency. Everything was so bureaucratic with them and they had little flexibility. They also had a full stores yard while our sapper one was always empty; once we obtained stores like concrete mix and blocks, we immediately started to use them. So, I am slightly ashamed to say that I turned a blind eye to when my sappers 'borrowed' stores from the UN, because I knew *we* were going to use them, not store them.

What was our role as the Royal Engineer Field Squadron?

We sappers were to provide engineer support to maintain roads; build bridges; provide drainage and culverts; generate electricity and fortify and protect UN and army installations. This enabled the infantry to guard checkpoints, convoys and installations, whilst allowing the cavalry to patrol Main Supply Routes (MSRs) and monitor all traffic.

It meant that the Field Troop was extremely busy doing a lot of building work in the local area, while the Support Troop spent much of its time spread out across the local area, maintaining the roads, many of which were no more than forestry tracks, so that the UN supply truck convoys could reach the local people that needed basic supplies like food, shelter, medicine and proper water. The quote from Nehemiah at the beginning of the chapter gives some insight as to how the Field Troop worked.

Nor were there just British Army units in the sector. These nationalities ranged from the Turkish Battalion (TurkBatt), the Pakistani Battalion (PakBatt), the Ukrainian Battalion (UkBatt), the endearingly abbreviated Bangladeshi Battalion (BangBatt) and the Malaysian Battalion (MalBatt). The Nordic units, (ScanBatt) were superb. Many others did not always impress as military units and the worst were derisively known as "Flip-flop Batt" because of their lack of military professionalism in the eyes of UK soldiers. When the rest of our Germany based engineer regiment arrived in late Spring for their Operation Grapple deployment, we were known collectively as BritEngBatt.

The military prowess of each one varied; the Turkish soldiers being one of the few that my sappers rated. On one occasion, when there was snow on the ground, I was going to a task with one of the Field Sections, in their vehicle. En route, I had called into Brigade Headquarters for some information. We parked the vehicle, a Saxon wheeled armoured personnel carrier, just inside the entrance and I left the Field Section in the back so that they could not get into mischief.

Or so I thought. Ten minutes later, I emerged from Brigade HQ to find my Field Section engaged in a very energetic snowball fight with the Turkish peacekeepers who were supposed to be on standby as a quick reaction force in case of local trouble. The whole battle ceased immediately on my appearance, with Turks and sappers alike either freezing like statues in the position they were in, or quickly dropping their snow missiles, putting their hands in their pockets and whistling badly. I felt like a Victorian Headmaster surprising an unruly classroom. I kept a straight face, though it was too funny for words, and gently asked my sappers:

'OK, fellas, shall we get back to work?'

Without a word, they piled back into the truck like a shot, but enjoyed good relations with the Turks throughout the rest of the tour.

We had been led to believe that the deployment was Spring-Summer-Autumn and would be warm, but being a Germany based field squadron, to a man we all thought it prudent to bring warm kit, just in case. Just as well we did. Two weeks after we arrived, the snow came, about 18 inches of it and it and stayed for another month.

Still, under our OC we had got into a busy routine early on and for the first few weeks of the tour, worked for 24/7 to begin to make some impact on local infrastructure.

In the early stages, this meant repairing potholes, culverts and drains by hand so that they did not fill and block up with water again. So, my Field Sections did the jobs properly, rather than by just shovelling gravel into the hole and hoping for the best. They needed no incentive to do it right from me, by the way, and were happy to work and 'leave their name on it'. Staff Smith was excellent at checking standards and pushing our squadron logistics to get the stores we needed, such as sandbags, wire, wood and all the other things that you can easily obtain in a local builder's merchants, but not in up-country Bosnia under UN administration, recovering from civil war.

Our first decent Field Section task was to re-deck a demolished little footbridge so that local school kids could get to school on the other side. There was still thick snow on the ground and the river was starting to flow full. The Corporal in charge, a cheery East Anglian, rightly reckoned that too much debris was building up on the bridge supports, so being a Field Section of rugged sappers, they took turns to get into the freezing waters and remove the rubbish. We had no idea what manner of unpleasant things lurked beneath, but they still just got on with it. It reminded me of Napoleon's 1812 winter retreat from Moscow, when his Dutch sappers worked for days in the frozen river to build a bridge at Berezina to enable the remnants of Le Grande Armee to escape Russia.

Many of the Field Section sappers stripped to their underpants and put on the camouflaged Gore-Tex trousers over the top, so that they had dry trousers to put on afterwards. Except one. Despite considerable pressure, he retained his combat trousers in the freezing water. When asked why, and expecting an answer about modesty etc., we were rewarded with the more honest response:

'It's because I ain't got no underpants on!'

Collapse of his Field Section in helpless mirth. I wonder what Nehemiah would have made of that?

The guys also had an anti-tank mine go off near where they were working, to which they reacted in their own words, 'Well, we all froze, bent our knees and looked at each other!' And work continued.

The Field Section did a great job at decking the old bridge, with handrails and made it look good. Stores were starting to arrive, aided by some dogged badgering by a determined Staff Smith.

By now the sappers had attracted quite a crowd of local people to their work (they had since put their trousers back on) and so when all was finished the local mayor came to open the bridge. He stunned us all by turning up in a 4x4 and driving it straight over the bridge, with bare inches either side of his tyres. Thankfully the bridge held, the local people were happy and their kids could go to school. Sadly, in under a week the handrails had all been nicked, but the bridge was still being used by the kids.

Our stock rose. Other tasks started to come the Field Troop's way. One was to set up the foundations on a high mountaintop for a Motorola relay station to be established to improve radio communications. I was tasked to recce and site the foundations, ready for a potential Field Section Task. It appeared a remote, complicated job. I took a Lance Corporal, the most qualified brick layer and concreter (who was trained in foundation work) from my Field Troop, together with the necessary concrete blocks on which the portacabin would sit and began to work out how to get there. I needn't have bothered; the pair of us were dropped off by a pre-arranged Navy helicopter on the top of the mountain and told 'See you in three hours.' And as the helicopter juddered away into the distance, we were left to it.

We were miles from, and miles above, anywhere. It was a solid, flat bedrock base, so no digging required. The relay station weighed tonnes. We simply laid out the blocks in the shape of the portacabin (I had the right dimensions in my trusty Aide-Memoire) on the rock and levelled them off so that they were even. He and I then looked at each other and we both said:

'Is that it?!'

There was no more work required; it had taken 10 minutes. So, we then sat, drank tea and chatted, perched high atop an outcrop of rock overlooking the stunning mountains of Bosnia-Herzegovina in the cold winter air and were collected by the helicopter at the agreed time. Not a bad morning's work.

As ever, fellowship was a challenge. There was an excellent British Army Padre, part of the Royal Army Chaplains Department, who was a strong believer and made every effort to regularly meet as many of the troops as he could every week. Bless him, he made a point of stopping by nearly every week for a time of fellowship and prayer. He was a great encouragement to me and perhaps had no idea how much his visits meant.

I also got into a good quiet time routine of getting up early and reading the Bible and talking to the Lord. And listening.

And speaking in tongues. It was a steadying discipline for this disciple. I found a dry, overhanging roof as part of an old disused building in the deserted corner of the camp that gave me privacy and meant I could go there whatever the weather. Set slightly apart from our accommodation, it ensured I was not disturbing anyone, or going to be disturbed myself.

This quiet time discipline is so vital for any Christian. It prepares you for the day ahead and helps you at least to start the day in a more Christ-like frame of mind (though we must continue to make good choices to abide there!). I also believe it enables the Lord to bless you without our even realising it sometimes. There is no such thing as fate or coincidence in our walk with the Lord and I know He delights to have time with us and He delights to dwell in us.

I also liked Christian as well as secular music, and had a Walkman with which I listened to tapes (no CDs yet!) of my favourite artists (Michael Card and Petra) because I found their music to be focussed on the Lord and the Bible instead of themselves. In particular, Petra inspired me because their lyrics consistently presumed that a Christian is there to speak up and not hide in the world, which struck a chord with my determination to stay true to Jesus. I realise now that I was keeping good stuff going into my soul, which all helps to keep walking with the Lord and not veer off course.

At the time though, all I knew was that I was responsible for thirty or so good blokes, none of whom I wanted to become casualties of accidents, mines or enemy action. I needed the grace of God to make decisions and to help me to manage the stress and the workload. Working in an environment where so many innocent people's lives had been wrecked or ended was quite wearying, too. Many of my sappers let off steam in our squadron bar, mainly at weekends because they took their working week seriously, but drunkenness was not an option for stress relief for a Christian like me. So instead, it was ensuring that every day I took some time to be with Jesus. And He helped me.

Of course, it was important to be in the squadron bar with the rest of the Field Troop, Support Troop and other squadron personnel. There was enough coke and orange for me to space out my beers with 'Muddy Puddle', and it was a good way of gauging how the blokes were doing. I enjoyed their company and the odd conversation about the meaning of life, once beer had loosened a few tongues again! Our bar was popular with the resident medical team too, and we reckoned it did no harm to be friends with the local health care.

Through all of this, Staff Smith was utterly invaluable as a sense check, idea-bouncer, and solid support. He never flapped, pointed out my faults respectfully, and kept firm but compassionate control of the Field Troop.

There were many local civilians working on site, helping to run the camp. There were also some keen young translators, whose bright university careers had been cut short by the civil war and who now were scraping a living helping us to communicate with the local leaders. I was busily pursuing my career in their country; I wondered when and if they would get a chance to pursue theirs.

I have never forgotten the medical centre swinging into action to treat a little boy who had been throwing stones nearby with some friends. Except that one of the stones had landed on an unexploded tank shell lying nearby, which detonated, causing horrific injuries to the boy which I will avoid describing to the reader. The guys in the Field Troop, exhausted though they were when they got back in the evenings, always took time to make a fuss of him, show him their guns and tools and let him play in and around the vehicles. Sappers have sometimes got bigger hearts than they want you to know.

Our contact with home was limited to one 20-minute phone-call a week, but unlimited free blue forces air mail letters. These 'blueys' were a lifeline and I wrote (and I think received!) loads. There was a rule that if you received more than ten in one day, you bought the lads a crate of beer. Well, one of my Field Section Commanders, a toweringly huge Scotsman, was occasionally considered by his Field Section to be mean with his cash when at the bar. Teasing him did not bring about the beers for which his sappers yearned, so they came up with a plan. They wrote and complained to his wife back in the base in Germany.

The next week, she responded, addressing ten simultaneous 'blueys' numbered 1/10, 2/10 and so on to her husband which all arrived on the same day. When opened in order they each contained one word of a sentence, which read: 'Get-the boys-a-crate-you-big-tight-scotch-Git.' The Field Section received its crate of beer that weekend.

Another aspect of life on an operational tour of duty were the photographs and letters sent by a wide range of females looking for pen-pals amongst HM Forces. Often photos were attached, some of which were pleasant and others of which left nothing to the imagination. They were distributed to sappers for them to arrange a liaison when they went home on leave. Sometimes the photos would be swapped out of a sense of mischief, leaving his so-called mates to speculate as to his reaction when the anticipated lady failed to match the expectation of the picture. This seemed harsh to me. I mention this because I wonder if the more well-meaning ladies who have tried to initiate a pen-pal or equivalent relationship with members of HM Forces ever had any idea of how their efforts sometimes were assessed and scrutinised.

Many of the sappers had nicknames, which prefixed their surnames. The Royal Engineers recruits across the UK, so many of their nicknames reflected where a guy was from. So, a Scotsman was 'Jock', a Welshman, 'Taff', and Ulsterman, 'Paddy' and so on. Within England, there were the usual nicknames, such as 'Scouse' from Liverpool, 'Brummie' from Birmingham and 'Geordie' from Newcastle. Anyone with red hair was often nick-named 'Ginge'. Those with surname Smith were nicknamed 'Smudge', White 'Chalkie' and so on. However, there was also plenty of cheerful inventiveness that went into a nickname.

I knew one sapper who was noticeably cross-eyed. His nickname was 'Uzzi', which was short for 'Who's-he looking at?'

I knew a passionate Welsh sapper in my Troop, from Swansea. He never missed a chance to explain how good it was in Wales and how much better Wales was than anywhere else; the sappers, growing weary of this, nicknamed him 'Jock'!

There was a Lance Corporal Noble, whose recruitment in the late eighties coincided with the nuclear explosion in Chernobyl, was nicknamed 'Chin'. And there was Sapper who just had a grumpy demeanour – his nickname was 'Attitude'.

There was a Sapper Kerr who was good at irritating people; his nickname was 'Wan'. On one of the Germany bases was a barmaid who was also cross eyed; she had one eye that looked down and another that stared fixedly ahead; her nickname was 'Dip and Dazzle'. And so on.

While it seems strange now to have described this aspect of army life, it does at least convey the strong humour and camaraderie that those who still serve there enjoy, and those of us who have now left miss the most.

As Christians, we must also aspire for that closeness of mutual trust and humour in how we do church. This sense of covenant must also be how we demonstrate fellowship to fellow believers and those yet to be believers. It must be genuine. Often as Christians, we do not consider ourselves to be in a warzone, whereas in effect we are. So, getting on with the Great Commission is one of our main objectives and we are not designed to do it alone. We have been commissioned to partner with God in restoring His planet, so we have lots to get on with.

In a place like Bosnia in the nineties where the infrastructure was in a poor state following the civil war, there was plenty for Royal Engineers to do, too. There were UN installations needing to be fortified, helipads to be planned and fuel installations to be sited.

It was a busy existence. My friend the Support Troop Commander and I would look at our opposite numbers amongst the infantry and cavalry officers and wonder if we were the mugs. We were working flat out keeping tasks going, whereas these guys seemed to just drive about, looking at things. Still, the tasks still needed planning and it meant you could save your money; I paid off my car loan for my Peugeot 306, because I was only really spending my money on 'Muddy Puddle', the odd beer and chocolate bars for six months.

And all this was against a backdrop of endless tasks. My third and final Field Section Commander, a dour Yorkshireman, proved adept at route repair, culvert building and ensuring that roads deteriorated less. So, this meant for good interoperability with Support Troop, whose Light Wheel Tractors were invaluable in saving a lot of leg work for my Field Sections.

As a Field Troop my unit was working really well together, and this also true within the squadron. The OC had succeeded in making his squadron efficient and determined, and greatly helped by Staff Smith and the Section Commanders, I believe the same could be said about my Field Troop.

Now it was time to raise the bar further, whilst continuing to look to Jesus.

Chapter 11 - Specific Prayer

James 5:16:

'The prayer of a righteous man is powerful and effective.'

Prayer is such a huge topic and this is not an attempt to write another book on the subject. However, the Bible is full of examples of where men and women are specific about what they are praying for and the Lord honours them. Think of Noah, Jeremiah, Nehemiah and Jesus. How many times were they disbelieved, laughed at, or persecuted for making a statement that challenged the faith of those around them? For taking a bold stance in the expectation that the Lord will actually do what a person asks of Him?

Perhaps this is because the person's stance of faith prickles the comfort zone of those they encounter. Perhaps the provocation causes hostility from the very people who should agree with, or be in support of, the person making the stand. And perhaps such people are not believed because those around them are, deep down, aware and uncomfortable about their own lack of faith.

When we are publicly specific about what we pray, or let people know about what we pray, God really does meet with us. In a church context, or in a Christian home, this is where a praying Christian can be encouraged to grow in their faith. The tragedy in the Bible is that so often, the home or equivalent church setting was where bold prayer was challenged, not encouraged. Jesus knew this from experience saying, 'A prophet has no honour in his own town,' in Luke 4:24. The story of Joseph takes its first dramatic turn when the boy not only has amazing dreams about himself and others, but has the boldness to share them. This provokes an ultimately murderous reaction, as Joseph found to his initial cost and eventual blessing in the Book of Genesis from Chapter 37 onwards. The ultimate biblical murderous reaction, of course, is the crucifixion of Jesus.

When a Christian takes a stand for the Lord in a pagan setting, the results can be impressive and memorable. A great example is Elijah's confrontation with wicked King Ahab in 1 Kings 17. This is where Elijah was publicly specific about what the Lord would do *before* He actually did it, in order to win back the Lord's disbelieving people. Another great example is David the shepherd boy describing the outcome of his contest with Goliath, to Goliath, before the 'contest' had even started. We Christians have a strong tradition from the Word of God to follow.

This can be quite intimidating, but we must start somewhere. Praying for parking spaces when sharing a car with an unbeliever is an example of a great place to begin this journey of faith. It can be bringing a Word of Knowledge or a prophecy to unlock a situation, or as simple as audibly asking the Lord to help you find the house keys, which I have had to do on many an occasion.

The applications and implications of this lesson are massive and I can only say that writing this now challenges me profoundly to practice what I preach more often. It unlocks faith in believers and reveals the living God to unbelievers. It challenges the static and encourages those who are moving for Christ.

It glorifies the Lord Jesus when our faith finds a public expression. Sometimes this is a public act of our choosing. Other times, desperation can cause an unplanned, yet heartfelt prayer of faith. I must admit to this happening in my life with great regularity, the 'Oh Lord, please help me in this situation to...' type of prayers with which I am all too familiar.

An example of this from my operational tour in Bosnia is a great testimony of how once again the Lord saved me from a mistake and potential disaster of my own making.

When sappers are not building bridges for the army, there are plenty of other battlefield construction tasks for them to do. One of the many projects I was given, while the Field Troop was getting on with the tasks that had already been planned (by me), was to prepare a landing site for helicopters to operate from, near our base in central Bosnia.

A suitable location, a field free from the endemic landmines of mid-nineties Bosnia, had been identified by the UN. The next stage was for a recce to be conducted by suitably qualified Royal Engineers to confirm its suitability for helicopter operations. This was simply a case of walking the ground to make sure it was generally firm enough for helicopters to land on and take off from. If not, the measures needed to prepare the planned airfield for operational use had to be identified, which include drainage, or putting down a concrete slab so that the ground is stable enough to handle helicopters.

Staff Smith and I were those suitably qualified Royal Engineers, and we spent an afternoon walking up and down the one kilometre square potential helicopter site, which was a beautiful level meadow of lush pasture typical of upland Bosnia. We found no obstacles, concealed wire, patches of marsh or hidden gullies which would be a hazard for flying operations. The ground was firm and well drained, even after rain and was going to be a suitable site for helicopters.

Of course, it was not the walk in the park that I describe. There was still a war going on and so we were each carrying loaded rifles, full magazines and our fighting equipment containing 120 rounds of ammunition in total. This was in case anyone took a pot-shot at either of us as we walked the potential airfield. Not ideal gear for an afternoon stroll, but vital for self-defence in a potential war zone.

As we completed the task, the sun was starting to dip towards the west and thoughts started to turn to the return to base, mealtime and a quiet evening. It was at that point that I realised with a sick-pit of-the-stomach feeling that somewhere in the field my rifle magazine had dropped off my rifle.

I do not mean losing a glossy colour supplement about firearms, but the piece of equipment which clipped to the underside of my rifle and contained 30 rounds of ammunition.

Losing this was a serious matter and a disciplinary offence. You cannot fire a rifle without ammunition, and it is hard to insist on high military standards amongst my soldiers if I, their officer and Troop Commander, could not keep hold of my own ammunition.

Earlier in the tour, one of my Corporals had lost a clip of ten rounds of ammunition somewhere in his accommodation. This left him with only 110 rounds until a frantic search for hours by him and his section revealed the missing clip, hidden in a fold of his webbing. He had visibly aged during the search because of the seriousness of losing ammunition. Thankfully for him the story had a happy ending. Except his nickname for the rest of the tour was 'Defender', after the 110 series Land Rover we used as a Royal Engineers' recce vehicle in Bosnia.

So, you can imagine the magnitude of losing 30 rounds. I asked my Staff Sergeant if he had seen a magazine of 30 rounds of ammunition on the ground somewhere in the field. His immediate answer rhymed with 'Oh clucking bell!' After a hard stare from him, he said words to the effect of 'Ohhh, great, Sir. Guess we had better find it, and fast.'

He and I started retracing our steps across this vast field, looking for the proverbial needle in the haystack. By now the sun was starting to set and Staff Smith was making helpful remarks like 'The light is failing, Boss.' and 'What are you going to do now?'

That was a good question. He was not being sarcastic. He and I knew that losing a magazine in a combat zone was, and is, a serious matter. He also knew the futility of trying to find a rifle magazine somewhere in a large grassy field with dusk approaching. I could not answer from within myself, so my only hope was to turn to someone who I knew could help.

'Well Staff,' I said, 'I don't know either, but I am going to ask God to help me to find it.'

And I did ask God, then and there in front of Staff Smith, to find my rifle magazine. Not a flowery prayer, but a very sincere one. My Staff Sergeant smiled in a somewhat cynical, slightly patronising way as you might expect. and we continued our search. For my part, I was trying to keep my faith alive. For his part, he was shaking his head sadly and tutting under his breath, which was infuriating.

Just then, an RAF helicopter from a base further down the valley flew overhead as we were walking the field. The low sun sparkled on the pilot's cockpit canopy whilst the crewman leant out and waved benignly at us as they clattered noisily overhead.

As it droned on over the end of the field it suddenly banked round to its left, as if it were about to land. To our surprise the pilot then touched the helicopter down at the end of the field so that the crewman could get out, reach the ground, and then get back in again. 'Looks like the field is suitable, Sir.' remarked Staff Smith with a puzzled expression as he tried to understand the helicopter's strange behaviour.

The helicopter lifted off before flying back the few hundred meters to land properly just beside where we were standing by the Land Rover. At that point, we had been considering whether to abandon the search and what the next course of action would be, and which senior officer needed to know. None of these were comfortable options from my point of view.

The crewman got out again and walked towards us, waving a small metal object. He called out 'Has anyone lost one of these?'

He was holding my missing magazine.

Just after I had asked for God's help, the helicopter had flown over the field. The low sunlight had reflected on the metal of the magazine and incredibly, the crewman had seen the glint from the helicopter a few hundred metres up. Why was he curious and persuaded the pilot to touch down and investigate? Why? God only knows!

Seeing me and Staff Smith walking up and down the field he had rightly assumed one of us had lost it; he was not surprised to see that it was the officer!

As I recall Staff Smith used words such as 'Jammy' when he had finished shaking his head and blinking with his mouth open.

But I was able to point out that I had prayed and that the Lord answered; there was nothing else he could say.

The Lord did it for me and He will do it for you.

Chapter 12 - The Rather Expensive Sentry Post

Luke 14:28-29:

'Suppose one of you wants to build a tower. Will he not first sit down and estimate the cost to see if he has enough money to complete it? For if he lays a foundation and is not able to finish it, everyone who sees it will ridicule him, saying 'This fellow began to build and was not able to finish.'

Drive by shootings were a recurring problem in Bosnia in the nineties.

What would happen was that a carload of young local men would accelerate past the guard post of a UN base or installation, firing a magazine of AK47 rounds in the general direction of the camp, the UN sentries and anyone else who happened to be in the way.

It did not cause many casualties, but the irritation factor was immense and the Brigadier wanted something done. He and the Brigade HQ were based in the town proper, unlike us on the town's outer rim in the factory complex and understandably his brigade staff had better things to occupy them than dodging random shots from adrenalin seeking local youths.

During the operational tour in Bosnia, the Brigadier decreed the construction of a solid sentry post on the flat roof of the Brigade HQ. From there, the Turkish UN peacekeepers who guarded

Brigade HQ could survey the whole area and perhaps return fire. If nothing else, the presence of a sentry box with such good visibility would make the 'drive by chancers' think twice.

As the resident Field Troop Commander, this landed in my so called 'in-tray', just as the snow was melting and just as the Field Sections were coping with all the damage suffered by waterlogged, overused, under designed Main Supply Routes (MSRs). 'I am afraid it needs sorting, Mark', was the OCs wry comment, 'He wants something solid up there, not some sandbag heap. You had best speak to the design engineers.'

The squadron was not the only Royal Engineer unit in the locality. In the Brigade HQ were a handful of other sappers, who had a design role and worked hard to design infrastructure projects that we could realistically deliver based on the stores available. Their boss, a very senior Captain and chartered civil engineer, welcomed me into their cramped office in Brigade HQ. Brigade HQ was an old factory, with numbers of military and UN personnel squeezed into a small spot and pushing a lot of paper around in circles as far as I could tell.

I sat down in front of his desk with the inevitable cup of tea, while he explained that my task was more complex than I thought. It was to look like a simple wooden sentry box, so that its rooftop location did not intimidate the more peace loving local people, yet needed solid protection from sandbags in case it was fired at. So, the design was wooden walls, internal and external, filled with compacted sandbags.

'Fair enough', I said, 'And just how am I going to get ten tonnes of sand up there?'.

'Oh, that's easy,' came the reply 'there is a fire-escape ladder going up the outside of the four walls of the building. Your sappers can take it up a bag at a time. They'll enjoy it!'

I begged to differ on that. Next question from me:

'And can the roof take the weight?'

'Yes, of course.'

I was not convinced and said so.

'Mark, I am the resident design engineer here. The roof can take the weight.'

'Well, if you are sure...'

'Mark, I am certain. Now if you'll excuse me, I have other matters going on...'

Clearly, the meeting was over, and I reported back to the OC, whose comment was 'Best get on with it then!' I was vexed though, at the prospect of my blokes having to shift a lot of sand up a high rickety ladder. Then my experience with the Motorola Relay station gave me an idea.

On the field, adjacent to the Brigade HQ (and clear of mines) was the Royal Navy helicopter detachment which had ferried me and the Lance Corporal up the mountain. They had a few Sea King medium lift helicopters, which were HM Forces workhorses in those days. Amazingly, in Bosnia there was little for them to do; the UN preferred to move stuff by land. The Royal Navy guys were, if anything, slightly bored.

So, I called in to see them, got chatting over another cup of tea and explained my predicament. I suggested my solution, which was to use the helicopters to lift the sandbags from the ground to the top of the building, where they could be lowered down to the right spot on the flat roof. The Navy fliers' eyes lit up. They *were* bored. They offered to train two of the sappers to safely unclip the sandbag loads at the top of the building and show the rest of the Field Section how to palletise the tonnes of sand so that it could go up in ten lifts of a tonne each.

Result!

To be on the safe side, I called back at the Design Engineers' office and checked my plan was acceptable. 'Sounds great. Just do it.' I was politely and airily waved away, as he plainly had more pressing matters to which to attend.

I told the OC what I was doing and whom I had spoken to; he was very happy at the 'out of the box' plan and that I had bothered to 'clear it' with the relevant authority.

A few days later all was set. The Field Section was trained and had palletised the sand, as well as the tools they were going to use, so that they didn't have to carry them up, either. Twelve lifts then. Two grinning sappers were atop the roof and nearby stood the rest of the beaming Field Section, pleased to not be having to work harder than the slaves who built the Pyramids.

The first Sea King helicopter started up, hovered into position and lowering the cable, was clipped to the first sandbag pallet. Effortlessly it lifted it off the ground and clattered the few hundred metres to deposit it safely on top of the factory. The sappers cheered, I was pleased and Staff Smith, who had come to 'help supervise', was enjoying the show, too.

The second lift was now taking place, exactly the same process as before, with the tools this time, all going without a hitch, with the Sea King roaring low over Brigade HQ to drop off the load.

At this point I noticed that the considerable downdraft generated by the helicopter rotors in such a confined space was having quite an unforeseen effect. Bins were starting to be blown over, and now the third lift was happening, their contents were being strewn across the Brigade HQ. Doors and windows were starting to bang and, as the fourth lift began, they were starting to break off. The bins were now blowing round by themselves, denting things. By the sixth lift, even some of the radio antennae were starting to bend at their mountings. But it was too late to stop now. Staff Smith tapped my arm, grimacing and trying not to smirk.

'Er, Troopy, I fink it's time we wasn't here. Back to the camp?'

I took his point. We quietly left and returned to our base, as the last lifts were dropped in and the Brigade HQ was consumed in a whirlwind of waste paper, looking like one of those New York ticker tape parades.

Later, I was called into the OC's office.

He was sitting at his desk, holding what looked like an invoice written in Serbo-Croat. This had the makings of an unusual interview question.

'Ah, Mark,' he began 'Well done on the sand moving at Brigade HQ, but you might want to be aware that the factory owner has presented a bill for $10,000 for damages caused during the helicopter operations. What would you like me to do with this piece of paper?'

'Well Sir,' I replied, 'Perhaps that's a question for the Design Engineer.' After all, he had said to me, 'Sounds great. Just do it.'

The OC pursed his lips, smiled and nodded. 'I agree. Let's leave it with him.'

Which he did and I heard no more about it. The UN was very good at reaching into its pocket to make problems go away, as the factory owner well knew. And it was therefore a rather expensive sentry post.

But there was yet more to this story.

The East Anglian Field Section Commander finished the job to an incredibly high standard, using a hollow timber frame which his section carefully filled with sandbags, so that the 'summer house' look of the sentry box was none the less well protected against flying bullets.

'Blimey Sir, this isn't force protection, this is a mick-take,' was the comment from the sappers, who were used to making far more sturdy, un-luxurious mini-fortifications on operations. Even the Corporal, who was a craftsman and loved building things, tongue in cheek asked if there was any lino spare with which he could finish the job properly. They even suggested having curtains, a vase of flowers and a doormat ready for when the Turkish soldiers took post.

The Brigadier was delighted with it, for its aesthetic appeal, good view for observing and firing and that the job had been done quickly. The cost was not mentioned.

The Turks took over, we left and continued to make a difference elsewhere. And that was that, or so we thought.

Some weeks later, after a period of very heavy rain, I had an urgent message from the Troop Staff Sergeant. He had been visiting Brigade HQ and wanted me to get down there immediately because there was a problem.

He met me at the HQ entrance and said, 'Come and look at this, Sir.' Water was pouring down the internal stairs of Brigade HQ. We ascended the flights of stairs, to the fourth floor, where the Brigadier had his accommodation. Water was pouring out from under his door. I looked at Staff Smith for an explanation.

One of his mates in Brigade HQ had tipped him off that there was a potential drama brewing. What had allegedly happened was that the Brigadier had stopped off at his accommodation a few hours before, to collect some things en-route to another meeting. On opening the door, he had been greeted by a mini tsunami. This has apparently had swept his bedroom slippers past where he stood at the threshold and on down the waterfall rapidly forming on the stairs.

We scrambled up onto the roof to investigate further. The heavy rain had created a pond up there because the Turkish sentries had not thrown their litter away but had shoved it down the only drain…which had blocked.

The heavy rain, with nowhere to go, had started to fill up the shallow flat-topped roof and a wide factory roof can hold a lot of heavy water. Which needed somewhere to go. I knew that from the story of the statue of General Gordon's camel. The combination of a sentry post weighing tonnes, plus a few more tonnes of water had been the straw that literally broke the camel's back (forgive the expression) and taken the roof load well over the maximum expected. The roof had cracked at its weakest point, just beside the sentry post and directly above the Brigadier's accommodation. And the water had made its getaway. Just like the camel, but a much more substantial flow.

Well, we quickly unblocked the drain, and raced back to the OC's office with the evidence. We also wanted to be the first with the news, lest a different version reached him from other sources.

And I am certain I was breathing those 'O Lord, please help me!' prayers with which I am familiar. And with which the Lord is also familiar.

Again, the OC listened and leant back in his chair. A mere sentry box was occupying quite a lot of his time, too. He surveyed the plug of Turkish sentry litter we had recovered, containing cigarette ends, lots of paper and a bag of washers which we couldn't explain.

'Well Mark,' he sighed 'I do recall that you checked that the roof could take the weight. So, I think once again, the Design Engineer is best placed to deal with this one.'

I heartily agreed and thanked the Lord for making another thorny problem go away.

And once again, I heard no more about it.

Then one day, at about the mid-point of the tour of duty, the OC sent for me. I knocked, saluted, and was invited to come in. He was holding a stack of plans and papers and looked up from his desk with a knowing smile.

'Ah, Mark, do sit down. I have a little job for you!'

Chapter 13 - When it is time to leave

Book of Ecclesiastes 3:1:

'There is a time for everything, and a season for every activity under the heavens.'

It is a good quotation because it is in the Bible and is therefore true. It has application in many situations, especially those which I am sharing of my experiences as a Christian officer in the British Army's Royal Engineers. In particular, it underlines how important it is to know when to stick around, and just as importantly, when to leave, at the appropriate time. The men of Issachar in the first book of Chronicles 12:32 knew the times, and Christians in the workplace should know this as well.

There have been many great books written about hearing God. Fundamentally it is about having the faith to do what you believe the Lord is asking you to do/say/think, when He is asking you to do it, irrespective of the reaction from others and yourself. This is a life skill which is developed by spending time with the Lord.

This includes reading the Bible, praying, praising, worshipping Him, speaking in tongues and fellowshipping with other Christians. The opportunity to apply our response to hearing God comes every day in a Christian's life.

A big challenge to hearing the Lord and 'knowing the time' can be success and a sense of one's own prowess...

pride. Symptoms include spiritual deafness based on increased self-confidence and reduced dependence upon the Holy Spirit.

There is a memorable point during my tour of duty in Bosnia where my growing confidence as a Royal Engineer Troop Commander led to me becoming rather full of myself. So, I will describe how I was brought back down to earth with quite a bump. This hard landing came from trusting in myself alone and choosing to not recognise good advice when it came, which led to me forgetting the golden rule of knowing the right time to leave.

The advice came from my excellent Troop Staff Sergeant, Staff Smith, who would not claim to be 'religious', but who had much experience, had 'been around' and was well placed to offer me wisdom.

However, this occasion springs to mind of when I chose not to follow his advice because some of my success had gone to my head. This occurred when having served a few months on the operational tour in Bosnia, I really began to think I was getting the hang of being an operational Troop Commander. My Field Troop and I had been doing well on the operational tour so far, with a strong sense of purpose, camaraderie and professionalism. Of course, I had much still to learn; Icarus was flying too close to the sun and pride does indeed come before fall...

* * * * *

Meanwhile, back in the office with the OC, I was wondering what he was going to say next and hoping it was good news from my perspective. Clearly pleased at having a decent sized task coming his squadron's way, the OC rubbed his hands together and told me the situation.

In the southern part of our Brigade sector, along one of the MSRs, there was a damaged concrete bridge.

The original bridge had suffered a demolition attempt by one of the warring factions, which had left it (the bridge, not the warring faction) weakened and in danger of further collapse. The bridge carried a critical MSR from the coast to the Bosnian interior, along which rolled the crucial UN supply convoys. The constant traffic of heavy good vehicles and UN armoured vehicles was causing the condition of the bridge to further deteriorate. Its collapse, aside from the obvious risk to life, would jeopardise the flow of humanitarian aid to a lot of needy people in Bosnia. A way had to be found to preserve the bridge before it collapsed and therefore keep the essential main supply route open. The bridge took the road over a 160-foot gap across a narrow valley and there was no other route available. A detour would have added hours onto UN convoy times and further clogged the already over-used Bosnian infrastructure. A solution had to be found.

The Royal Engineer design team in the local headquarters (they were still talking to me) came up with the simple idea of my Field Troop building an overbridge, an 'equipment bridge' *over* the bridge. This would carry the traffic a few feet above the existing bridge with room to spare from one end to the other. This meant that the supply route would stay open and that the weight of traffic was carried by the equipment bridge.

Once the overbridge was built and the load safely taken off the existing bridge, my Field Troop could then effect the repairs necessary to the original bridge so that once the concrete had hardened, the equipment bridge could be removed and used elsewhere in the sector and the existing bridge would be good as new. Simple.

As I had the honour of commanding the only combat engineer field troop in the sector, the task of constructing the overbridge and repairing the underbridge was mine.

This was a major challenge because this was a high-profile task requiring much planning and co-ordination in its preparation and delivery. I remember praying a lot at the time because I felt very intimidated by how much needed to be done. And the Lord answered because I found the whole process broke down into very logical steps, which enabled the task to be approached with realism, not optimism.

The first phase was the overbridge and then after that the second phase repairs for the original bridge sub-structure needed planning.

The preparation for the equipment overbridge was considerable. We needed to span the 180-foot gap, with two thirty-foot approach ramps at either end making it a 240-foot bridge to carry a forty-tonne articulated supply lorry. There was insufficient Royal Engineer bridging equipment available at that time in Bosnia. However, the squadron officers persisted and tried many avenues.

Eventually contact was made with the Overseas Development Agency, which had large quantities of a new type of equipment bridge called 'Mabey Johnson'. This was like Bailey Bridge, but as the sappers were to find, significantly heavier. However, it did mean that we could increase the load that the overbridge carried to seventy tonnes. Given how difficult it was to enforce law and order, let alone the weight limits of a bridge, a higher limit that was unlikely to be exceeded was a more sensible option. The Overseas Development Agency had sufficient Mabey Johnson equipment bridge for us and could deliver it very quickly by sea to the Croatian port of Split.

The build itself was planned for a few weeks' time, in June. It was to take place on a Sunday night, between 1800 hours and 0800 hours the following Monday morning. This would minimise disruption to the supply route, which ordinarily was open 24/7. But it would only leave my Field Troop a fourteen-hour window in which to start and finish the build; there would be no second chance.

Out of the whole Field Troop, only one Sapper and one Lance Corporal had ever used this type of bridge before and so getting familiar with the Mabey-Johnson equipment bridge was essential. After all, we only would have one opportunity to build it and get it right.

Staff Smith was very aware of this and strongly recommended the Troop practice the build to reduce the risk of mistakes. I knew both intellectually and in my spirit that this was a seriously good idea. We both could see the value of planning some 'dress-rehearsals' and so Staff Smith sorted this out almost immediately.

The rehearsals were arranged to take place in the city of Split, Croatia, where we had first arrived and because it was also the port where the bridge was to be delivered.

That week's rehearsal time in the Engineer Resources Park in Split would be invaluable for each member of the Field Troop to understand their part in the build and to ensure that they were familiar with the whole project, not just their own part. It also enabled us to check that we had all the parts needed so that nothing was missed out.

However, the planning and preparation was a task in its own right and deserves special mention here, because all too often a guy can bask in the success of others, which leads to pride… which can lead to a fall. One of the reasons for me writing this all down is to be very honest about the experiences the Lord has given me, to encourage other Christians on their walk with the Lord to listen to His voice and to not ignore good advice.

But often, good advice can come from unexpected sources. These can include people with no Christian faith at all. The Christian needs the wisdom of God, via the Holy Spirit, to weigh this. Failure to do this 'weighing' can have unforeseen consequences and it is a crucial life skill for any Christian to 'weigh' words, or a situation, with the wisdom the Lord gives. This helps a guy to know what to do and when to do it, as the above quote from Ecclesiastes shows.

Liaising with our squadron Quartermaster and his team, Staff Smith then arranged for the Field Troop to go to the Engineer Resources Park in the city of Split, Croatia, where the bridge we were to use was being unloaded at the docks. Staff Smith's rationale was to practice the build, using the actual equipment bridge with which we were to build, on a site that was like the crumbling bridge in Bosnia where it was to be built for real. This meant that the rehearsals for the operation were as close as possible to the real thing. This was so that the sappers would know what they were doing for the real-time build, which was limited to a 14-hour window, by night. This was a sensible, risk reducing approach and I whole heartedly agreed.

So, this is where my Field Troop and I trained for a few days to get it right. This had the advantage of being away from our base in Bosnia, so that all the Field Troop could concentrate on learning their part in the build and not be distracted. It also meant that if there were any parts missing in the equipment bridge, they could be more easily replaced in a large port such as Split, rather than leaving it until later when we returned to base, which was a town with a small UN base deep in the mountains of Bosnia. The equipment bridge would need well over a dozen large trucks to transport, to give you an idea of its scale.

The rehearsals took a week. After a slow first build to get used to the new equipment and ironing out snags, the second build went very well. All the kit was there, and it gave the Troop the opportunity to not just learn to build it but work out the best schedule for delivery of parts to the site from the stores area. This sounds very drab when describing it, but when the clock is ticking and it is dark, trying to fit the wrong section of bridge out of sequence is no laughing matter and can jeopardize the build. Which can jeopardize the bridge. Which means no UN relief convoys can get through. Which means innocent people suffer, and in some cases, die, for the want of the UN supplies that the convoys are carrying. Getting it right in rehearsals *is* important.

Now that my Field Troop had the sequence of construction nailed, it was a case of improving the speed of build. This type of equipment bridge was new to the Royal Engineers and most of us had not used Mabey Johnson bridges before. However, sappers are well motivated quick learners who are proud of their craft and all of us applied ourselves to becoming familiar with the new bridge. Mabey Johnson is very similar to Bailey Bridge and so my TA experience of a few years before came in very useful to help me understand how it all fitted together and how difficult it could be to assemble at night in a hurry.

We knew that the 14-hour window was important, because we were in effect blocking the supply route during that build. I needed the assurance that we could complete the task within the time frame and it was vital that all of us, not just me, had an idea of just how much bridging kit is required to cover a 240-foot span.

But everyone has their specific part to play – I was responsible for the plan and the overall operation. Staff Smith had to control the construction of the bridge itself, which meant working closely with the rest of the Troop. The Troop was already divided into its sections, each commanded by a Corporal, as 'left of bridge', 'right of bridge' and 'centre of bridge' for the construction of the equipment bridge. They and the sappers did the hard graft of building the bridge.

The bridge we were building was 240 feet long, so you can see that there were a lot of 'four-man', 'six-man' and 'eight-man' lifts in a bridge of that size and you get an idea of the hard work involved in assembling it. Thankfully, my Field Troop were all fitter than a butcher's dog and had certainly not gone to seed in Bosnia.

On the final build of the week, my Field Troop built the 240-foot overbridge in just under 11 hours, which was well within the 14-hour time window needed for real during the operational build. The rehearsals had gone successfully, and we were pleased with ourselves.

On the last day Staff Smith suggested that a few beers out in the town the evening before we set off back up country to Bosnia would be a good way of saying 'well done' to the boys. There was no town as such to have a beer near the base in Bosnia. This suggestion seemed fair enough, and so I agreed.

So, that evening, off we all went to a local hostelry. A few beers were being 'quaffed' and the boys were enjoying themselves. The bar was somewhere in downtown Split, and more like 'Rovers Return' than Wetherspoons, but it was friendly enough. There was much laughter and noise, in the cheerful, raucous atmosphere in which British soldiers excel when they are behaving themselves. The fact that the few locals present had not left told me that no offence was being taken at the sappers' boisterousness; so far, so good and I started to relax, too.

However, a little later in the evening the door opened and in came a group of Croat soldiers. They were clearly locals, and from their body language and interaction with the bar staff, they were fresh from the frontline of their ongoing war with Serbia. At that time, the war upcountry between Croatia and Serbia was in full swing, with some nasty atrocities still taking place.

Ignoring us Royal Engineers, the Croat soldiers sat themselves down at the far end of the room and ordered beer. A lot of beer. They were equivalent in number to us and were minding their own business. And so the evening developed, with two social events developing at either end of the bar, but with no problems and some humour in evidence.

After an hour or so, Staff Smith looked round the room, then leant across to me and indicating just the two of us, quietly urged 'Sir, it is about time us two went.'

I looked at the two relatively benign groups of soldiers, and aware that I was just starting to relax (for the night was still young) said:

'I am just starting to enjoy it Staff, it seems a shame to go so early.'

He shook his head and looking knowingly at the Croat soldiers busily guzzling beer at the other end of the bar, sucked his teeth and not-so-quietly urged:

'No sir, you are not listening to me. It really is time we went.'

I smiled. I was growing in confidence. I was becoming a very accomplished Troop Commander and self-assured. The evening was very pleasant, and the 'crack' and banter was a relief after some very long days. I said as much to Staff Smith and he gave me a bleak look.

'Sir,' he murmured through clenched teeth. 'You don't get it. It is now time for us to leave and let the boys have their fun.'

Well, the boys were not urging us to leave as far as I could tell and so I shook my head with sublime confidence. After all, I had become a very good Troop Commander.

'It's fine Staff,' I breezed 'Everything is OK and those Croats over there are quiet enough – I will leave later.'

My window of opportunity was closing fast and I was not listening to the Holy Spirit, that still small voice which warns you when you are somewhere you should not be, and need to go to where you should be.

Staff Smith sighed deeply, raised his eyebrows and frowned before getting up.

'Well, I will see you later then, *Sir*,' was his parting shot (with a twist of sarcasm in the word 'Sir') as he stalked out of the bar, shaking his head slightly.

He headed back to our UN accommodation in Split where the Troop had been based for the week.

Barely five minutes had elapsed before one of the Corporals came across to me. He will remain nameless but had clearly enjoyed a lot of local beer.

'Shirr,' he rasped beerily to me in his Welsh valleys' drawl before nodding at the Croats at the other side of the room 'See those boys thurr? They don't seem to be finding us boys yerrr funny anymore.'

He had a point. The Croats were definitely not appreciative of the singing and japes that were evidently amusing the Royal Engineers present. I turned back to the Corporal and shamelessly suggested 'Perhaps it is time we went?'

'Nah, we will be alright boss, we is Royal Engineers' was the reply from the Corporal, who with hindsight was clearly not yet ready for the role of Troop Staffy. But he was also not ready to overlook what happened next.

Suddenly, with no warning, one of the surlier looking Croat soldiers, who could easily have been mistaken for an extra from 'Planet of the Apes', leapt to his feet, grabbed a lamp that happened to be standing nearby, and brought it down hard across the shoulders of one of the stockier sappers in my Troop as he emerged from the gents' toilet.

However, the sapper did not crumple, to the Croat's evident surprise; he looked at the dented lamp he was still holding with a perplexed expression because there was no visible dent on the sapper. An unexpected outcome for the Croat. Knowing the sapper, who had the physique of a Narnian Ogre, I was not surprised.

There was a pause of about two seconds before the Corporal yelled a brief, urgent call to arms, punctuated with some unrepeatable expletives, to the rest of the Troop. A rough translation is as follows:

'Forsooth, yonder Croat fellow has assaulted one of our number. A fell act, with no prior warning, which requires a response from all of us Royal Engineer soldiers here present. Gentlemen, we have a wrong to right, requiring us here gathered to express our collective indignation at such an unprovoked act and ensure it is not repeated.'

Whereupon the whole troop, as a baying pack of hounds, fell upon the rapidly mobilising group of Croat soldiers and a battle royale erupted in the bar. I quickly realised that British soldiers with their blood up, a skinful of beer, an enemy in front of them and an attack to avenge are not responsive to conventional officer-like command and control in the way that one is trained to expect at officer training at the Royal Military Academy, Sandhurst. My raised voice, pointing out that this was not a good idea and that some-one was going to get hurt, had no effect on the situation whatsoever.

In fact, I was exercising zero command and zero control, as the punches started to fly. Then one of the Croats flew too, being propelled over the bar by some Royal Engineer muscle before landing in a protesting, then unconscious, heap by the entrance to the back door. My plaintive attempts to halt the proceedings and calm my sappers were utterly ineffectual; indeed, I can only claim the Lord's protection as to why I was not decked and felled by a raging Croat wanting to strike a blow.

Before very long, it was clear that the Royal Engineers were gaining the upper hand in what was a toughly fought contest, but the final outcome will never be known because the sound of a police siren had the calming effect that my well-intentioned protestations had not achieved. Both sets of protagonists paused in unison and as one man decided that flight was better than fight. The reputation of the Croat police at that time was hardly one of passive restraint. The bar was emptying rather fast and so I concluded that my presence was no longer necessary, either.

The flying Croat's unplanned landing zone by the back door had indicated a clear escape route and so I vaulted the bar, and the still recumbent Croat, like a champion triple jumper and was away out via the fire exit in the blink of an eye. A pause to ensure that the police were all entering the front door and then a brisk walk down the back alley to the main street before making my own way back to the accommodation. I had no idea of the fate of my soldiers and there was quite a commotion in the bar; but there were no tell-tale Anglo-Saxon oaths (or

Welsh/Irish/Scottish ones, either) which indicated that the Croat police were only arresting the home side on this occasion.

I returned to the accommodation as quickly as possible without drawing attention to myself and roused Staff Smith from his sensible slumber. The implications of the evening's events were starting to dawn on me, and my earlier self-assured swagger was no longer evident.

Staff Smith sat up and heard my account. He then asked for a repetition and checked two key details:

1. No sapper arrested that I knew of.
2. No sapper in hospital that I knew of.

He then looked at me rather hard for a moment. I did not know what to say. He knew he did not have to say anything, not even 'I told you so.' He merely murmured

'We'll sort it out in the morning at parade,' before rolling back into his sleeping bag.

I was left to ponder. We had two very different nights after that. Staff Smith slept like a log, snoring as would a well-fed badger. Meanwhile, I took counsel of my fears, and barely slept a wink. I was imagining my court martial and the implications of my failing to prevent a diplomatic incident in a region already at war with itself. I lay there, also wondering if any of my soldiers were enduring the hospitality of the Croat police. What would my OC and CO say? Would I be dishonourably discharged? And so on. A far cry from the smug, self-confident young Troop Commander at the beginning of the evening. I know I prayed a lot, and I repented too because I knew my pride had implicated me in an incident that humility would have spared me. It was a long night.

Believe me, I was ready on parade the next morning and so was the rest of the Troop. They were all formed up in three ranks and from a distance looked like normal soldiers. Closer inspection revealed black eyes and bruises, together with the tell-tale swaying, like tall trees in a gale, of hung-over, bruised British soldiers trying to stand to attention.

I did not know what to say to them, but I was in the process of forming some kind of speech when a quiet 'Ahem' from behind me revealed that Staff Smith was ready to address my Troop of sappers first. But before he did that, he said to me in a quiet voice:

'Sir, would you go and have a look at the tyres on the trucks and check they are alright?'

Now officers are not normally asked to do vehicle inspections by their staff sergeants, but even in my shattered state I took the hint. It was that he wanted to speak to the men without the awkwardness of an officer like me being present. I had no moral high ground upon which to stand that morning of all mornings. And I had already decided that I was going to take good advice from now on with no argument. So, I agreed that it would be a good idea for me to check the transport and so I walked to the waiting lorries as requested.

However, there was a gentle breeze that morning and it carried his words to me as I went through the charade of checking the tyres. So as Staff Smith addressed our sappers, I overheard an exchange of information which I have never forgotten:

Staffy: 'Right you lot, you are all here, but you look terrible. Are there any serious injuries?'

Field Troop: 'No, Staff.'

Staffy: 'Anyone arrested, missing?'

Field Troop: 'No Staff.'

Staffy: 'Right. Listen carefully, all of you. Last night never 'appened. I was not there. The Troop Commander *most definitely* was not there. And like I said, last night never 'appened. Any questions?'

Field Troop: 'No Staff.'

Staffy: 'Right, let's get on the wagons and go.'

Field Troop: 'Yes Staff!'

And that was it. I had no comeback about it and we returned to camp without incident.

I had reaped some rapid consequences of my pride that evening. Pride does come before fall, but after fall I learned afresh that the Lord hears repentance, too, and He forgives. I had every reason to expect to have to answer for my culpability in that situation, but the Lord covered it for me; He is so good and faithful. Incidentally, I was also foolish to have worried all night after the fight, because there was nothing else I could do – I allowed myself to be robbed of a night's sleep through worry (and I repented of that, as well).

Some way into the six-hour journey back to our base in Bosnia, I was lost in contemplation of the lessons learnt from the night before. The rest of the sappers were fast asleep, and I was starting to drift off myself. Staff Smith called across to me with his familiar lop-sided grin and said, 'You know somefink Boss?'

Well, I didn't, but the more familiar 'Boss' rather than the formal 'Sir' told me that he felt I had learnt my lesson and that my rehabilitation was well underway.

'You know' he went on, 'It's good skills – the boys stuck together, they fought together and they won. You can't ask for more than that from the soldiers you lead, can yer?'

He was making a very good point and I had to accept that fighting together and winning is what soldiers train to do. 'You are quite right, Staff,' I agreed. It was time to put the events of the last night behind me and get on with the job in hand, of commanding a Royal Engineers Field Troop. But this time, open to more help from the Holy Spirit…and Staff Smith!

Ultimately, the Lord rescued me from my proud stupidity and my sensible Staffy brought a very British Army solution to the problem too. And over twenty years later, I continue to try to listen to the Lord, and do what He says at home, in the workplace and at church…all the time. When He says it. Irrespective of what I think or what others might think about the outcome.

Which means I am much better at knowing when it is time to stay…and when it is time to leave.

Chapter 14 - Overbridge

Proverbs 3:5-6:

'Trust in the Lord with all your heart and lean not on your own understanding,
In all your ways acknowledge Him and he will make your paths straight.'

With the success of the bridge build rehearsals and my salutary lesson in humility, I was in a very good place to take the above quotation from the Book of Proverbs to heart and actually apply it. Without realising this at the time, I was trying to copy what Nehemiah had done, when he had understood what the Lord had asked him to do, faced down his fears, and tried to make it happen.

Like Nehemiah, I could only thank the Lord for enabling me to embark on a project that was well beyond my natural ability.

The bridge needed a dozen huge army lorries to transport it all back up to our base in Bosnia, where it was stored for the great day. We made sure nothing was left behind!

However, the worsening tactical situation meant that the day was delayed, throwing out the carefully planned leave arrangements of my Field Troop. More Mabey Johnson bridge building training took place in a hastily cleared area in our squadron base, this time for the sappers who had hitherto expected to miss out on the build. Those who had trained, but were going on leave without building the final bridge, were gutted. This proved again that the first rehearsals in Split had been vital, by now because my sappers knew the bridge very well, and not just their own part of it.

The building of the overbridge took a lot of planning. I ended up writing twelve pages of orders for the operation, because placing a 240-foot bridge in the middle of a heavily used UN MSR in a single night was going to affect a lot of people.

Obviously, my Field Troop needed to know what was happening, but not just on the bridge building site. They also needed to know what was happening beyond the site, so that they could concentrate on the build and not have anything else about which to worry. The orders had to include instructions for the drop-off of the eleven huge pallet loads of bridge, in the right order, so that the bridge could be properly assembled in the dark. There were the orders for reporting progress to squadron HQ, and then on to the UN HQ and Sector HQ. Visitors from the UN needed to know where to stand, because you cannot have senior people wandering round an equipment bridge building site unsupervised; they may get hurt.

The orders also had to include the UN liaison officers; they needed to pass on this information to the local population so that they did not use the route at that time and understood what the purpose of the overbridge was. The military police needed to know, in order to limit military traffic. It was important that the local British infantry company, UN peacekeepers like us, knew the situation so that they could adequately protect the site, lest the prospect of a concentration of UN-dressed sappers proved too much of a temptation to any trigger-happy locals. Local media had to be made aware as well, because this was a 'good news' story that the UN wanted to use to advocate the benefits of peace. The site also had to be checked for mines (none were found). I prayed and planned; and then did a lot of writing.

It is no good giving orders if they are not understood, so the OC suggested I took all those commanders and representatives who needed to be involved to the site a few days before and 'walk the ground' before giving the orders. It was good advice.

I took the group of them to where the damaged bridge was and conducted a 'walk through, talk through' with the commanders and representatives so that they all saw the bigger picture and were clear of their part in the overall plan. Everyone saw where the bridge would go and how little space there was in which to work; everyone was 'up for it!'. In today's management jargon, I was able to 'secure wider team and stake holder buy-in.'

I then gave the formal orders to nail down the timings and a day or so later, everything and everyone moved to the bridge site. It was now D-Day. The Mabey-Johnson equipment bridge pallets were carefully located on the approach road to the bridge site as planned and the Field Sections were in position. Staff Smith stood nonchalantly at the near end of the bridge, arms folded, waiting for the green light. At 1800 hours I was notified that the MSR was now closed and that we were free to build. We were underway!

The Field Troop worked its way steadily through the evening, with its three component Field Sections being 'left of bridge', 'right of bridge' and 'centre of bridge' respectively. My ever-reliable Troop Staff Sergeant Smith controlled the build for what would be a long night. There was not much noise; the guys just got on with it.

In many respects, my job was complete once I had given the orders, though in reality, I knew Staff Smith needed me to keep 'tourists' away and out from under his feet during the build. So, I quietly intercepted the inevitable stream of senior military officers and UN officials who came to visit the spectacle. I stood there explaining what was going on and talking with them, while my Field Troop did the hard work.

In my mind's eye I can still see the site, this illuminated pool of hard-working sappers, set against the backdrop of the forest clad Bosnian mountains with the river raging beneath. I can still hear the quiet words of command 'hands on...lift!' as the respective section commanders of left of bridge, right of bridge and centre of bridge assembled their part of the bridge section in turn.

They only stopped for brief breaks to drink. I remember one such break coinciding with a late visit from a senior British officer, and as I formally briefed him about the project, two of my sappers did a quick dance routine in my line of sight (but out of the senior British officer's) to try and make me laugh.

It grew dark. It was a warm, dry Bosnian summer night and the squadron Quartermaster had thoughtfully provided floodlights which illuminated the scene dramatically, attracting thousands of moths and glow-flies, which added interest to the occasion.

The Field Troop made great progress, working steadily through the night as section by section the bridge grew in length, gradually spanning the gap as the light faded and went. However, a mini-disaster struck when one of the two jacking-handles was dropped by a sapper into the gap, never to be seen again. The jacking handle was needed to adjust the height of the bridge at each stage of the build. Loosing 50% of these key items was not good news. This did not endear the culprit to the rest of the Field Troop, some of whom felt he should have followed the handle head first into the gap for his mistake.

But we were still on track. By the small hours there were no more visitors, surprise, surprise and the challenge was to finish the bridge on time. Which the thirty sweating sappers did, just after 5am, so with nearly three hours to spare. Fantastic!

The news was passed on via our radio link and as the first rays of the sun illuminated the mountaintops far above our heads on the Monday morning, the MSR was re-opened.

The guys were exhausted, as you might imagine. We gathered at one end of the bridge for the inevitable troop photograph to celebrate.

We had the site to ourselves and could soon expect the first UN convoy. One of the Corporals asked Staff Smith about checking whether the new equipment bridge would really take the load? Quick as a flash, two of my sillier sappers leapt to their feet, dropped their trousers et al, and ran the length of the new bridge with their trousers round their ankles, their buttocks bared, shouting 'It works! It works!' as they did so.

Never a dull moment.

So, it all went very well, with the Sector Commander, the affable British Army Brigadier (the one who had been recommended promotion for his excellent fire control order and who had also recently become a flood victim!), being very effusive in his praise for my Field Troop, for our squadron, and Royal Engineers in general.

It was understood that he had grown rather frustrated by the complexities of international co-operation with the different national armies representing the UN. So, when a British Army unit delivered a high-profile major task on time and without problems, the Brigadier was naturally very pleased that he had not been let down by his home team.

Meanwhile, I had a lot for which to thank the Lord. So much can go wrong on a build like that, and it did not. It went right. No one was injured and we did what we had set out to do. I simply had to trust the Lord at every stage and especially on that night build. Given that Nehemiah had worked round the clock, too, I am sure he would have approved.

The construction of the overbridge was a massive undertaking, and my soldiers who did the hard work of building the overbridge would cry 'Amen' to that. The planning and delivery of it was a professional highlight for me.

It was viewed as a great feather in my cap and very useful for my CV, though I must add it did involve a lot of hard work by others as well as me.

Practice, practice and yet more practice building the bridge at the Engineer Resources Park in Split and again at our Bosnian base had paid dividends in making sure that the actual bridge build took place with a minimum of hitches on the night.

But I know that trusting the Lord with all my heart and not leaning on my own understanding had made my paths straight, and provided a decent overbridge, too.

Now it was time to deal with the existing bridge itself.

Chapter 15 - The Underbridge and a Spot of Leave

Philippians 4:13:

'I can do all this through him who gives me strength.'

During the build-up to constructing the overbridge, I was very aware that it was only half of the project and that there was a sizeable task awaiting to repair the existing bridge from its war damage. I knew what had to be done, but supply constraints were to delay progress with completing this.

The bridge was of a reinforced concrete construction, so the first task was to break out all the damaged concrete and bar so that, in the words of a car salesman, we 'knew what the damage was.' Once the sappers had done that, we could set up new formwork in the original shape of the bridge and pour in new concrete, with reinforcement, so that the bridge would be as good as new.

Within the Field Troop were all the joinery, concreting and other construction skills necessary to do the project. This is where the Royal Engineer 'trade' skills became so valuable.

One of the challenges was having to dam the river, by hand, to make a sandbag cofferdam so that the concrete pour to the bridge arches could take place. The sappers just ignored the physical hardship and got on with this labour-intensive way of overcoming the river.

Sadly, the main problem was delivery of stores provided by the UN. This meant that deadlines kept being missed again and again, and so the works schedules were being forever delayed. Personally, this was frustrating because I had really hoped that we would finish the bridge completely, but that was not to be. The days were spent ensuring that the sappers had enough meaningful work with which to continue, whilst hoping that the promised concrete, wood and stores would arrive on time from the UN. Which they did not. Meanwhile other taskings came in which required me and Staff Sergeant Smith to juggle our workforce; I daresay operational tours with the Royal Engineers can often be like this!

This can be a hard lesson. On one hand, I knew that the Lord had enabled me and my field troop to achieve significantly more than we thought. And yet when I read the Book of Nehemiah, it is as if it ends prematurely, halfway through his work to restore not just Jerusalem's walls, but the people as well. So, I consoled myself that I was in good company, and that like me, Nehemiah had been blessed with some very capable operators who had helped him to accomplish more than perhaps even he expected.

We ended up handing over the project to the next Royal Engineers Field Squadron to take our place in Bosnia, just as the UN stores were finally starting to arrive.

Still, it did mean that the Field Troop set up a tented site near the bridge so that at least two out of three Field Sections could get on with breaking concrete, setting up formwork, building cofferdams and any other tasks associated with repairing the underbridge.

The guys really enjoyed the independence and worked hard. Staff Smith stayed there a lot of the time to maintain momentum and I commuted from the squadron base. It was not ideal from my point of view, but my OC had other jobs for me to do; in his opinion spending all my time on the bridge site was not the most effective use of my time as Troop Commander.

Then, a body blow; Staff Sergeant Smith was posted! He was to take up an appointment as a QMSI in a Royal Engineers territorial army regiment back in the UK and was to leave the squadron a month or so before the end of the tour.

Staff Sergeant Smith was everything a Troop Staff Sergeant should be: loyal, professional, wise, humorous and a fountain of knowledge and good counsel to a Troop Commander like me. I always think of him as one of the best soldiers I have ever met and a Christmas card every year does not adequately convey my ongoing gratitude for his pragmatic encouragement during one of the most potentially challenging periods of my life.

I was very disappointed to lose him, as you might imagine, but that is the way it goes in the Army. I had one of the squadron recce sergeants step into the role of Field Troop Staff Sergeant until the end of the tour and it worked very well. This would be my fourth 'Troop Staff Sergeant' in 18 months. He came from an airborne background like Staff Sergeant Smith and as my OC remarked,

'Well Mark, you are just swapping one ugly paratrooper for another!'

Meanwhile, the Mabey Johnson overbridge coped very well with transferring the load from the road. I was on hand to witness a 'nose to tail' convoy of British Army (in UN markings) Warrior Armoured Fighting Vehicles using the overbridge in a hurry when the tactical situation in Bosnia worsened. No damage to the bridge!

On a happier note, with the overbridge complete and the underbridge phase now planned and starting, it was now my turn for leave and Rest and Recuperation (R&R) a fortnight after the midterm point. I was well and truly ready for it.

Back then, a UK soldier in a UN zone on an operational tour was also entitled to three or so days R&R as well as the usual two week leave slot. The standard practice was to have three days R&R down on the Croatian Coast, near Split, before taking the two weeks' leave.

The reason for doing it like this was cynically explained to me. It was deemed better for guys to let off steam on the Croatian Coast for a few days out of harm's way, rather than back at home on leave. In these days before counselling became more common place, this had a certain brutal military logic.

The three days R&R was memorable in many ways.

Certainly, the group of Royal Engineers from both squadron and Field Troop had a lot of steam to let off. They had been working long hours, under the constant threat of someone potentially wanting to shoot at them. They had money in their pockets. They were looking forward to getting home.

The little Croatian seaside town may not have previously enjoyed such a medley of rugby songs, military ditties and drunken tra-la-la-ing as when it was R&R time that first evening. The few outside bar areas in that idyllic cobbled town square were full of Royal Engineers, all busy 'de-stressing'. I knew many of them and by that time the rest of the engineer regiment had deployed to Bosnia, so it was not just personnel from my Field Troop and squadron taking their turn to go on leave.

In fairness, it was all good humoured and the boys were generally behaving themselves. Yet we were not the only nationality represented in the square that evening. A few yards away sat a group of very large Canadian peacekeepers, who were also due for their R&R. They were stony-faced and not looking at all impressed at the Royal Engineer tomfoolery that they were witnessing; perhaps they did not know all the songs.

The evening progressed, with more noise and song, and further consumption of alcohol. Remembering my experience of the bridge rehearsal week and while it was still relatively early, I was preparing to leave and let the boys play. Before I could do so, one of the Canadians cleared his throat and snarled at a table of sappers:

'You Brits are all noise and no action. You are not even funny.'

An immediate, shocked silence descended. The appallingly provocative nature of the remark surprised everyone, including the other Canadians.

Thankfully, there were a few SNCOs present, without whom I would not have rated the Canadians' chances against a town square full of provoked sappers. I was not the only officer present, either, but that did not affect what happened next.

The silence was broken by one of the vehicle fitters from the squadron, who was sitting nearby. With an indignant expression turned slowly round in his seat and faced the Canadian table.

'So y'think us ahr ahll boring then, do yuh?' he asked, in his broad north country tones. He received no answer from the Maple Leaf Table.

He then solemnly asked for a dining fork and a wine cork. He now had the attention of the entire town square.

Taking a lighter, he carefully burned one of the fork prongs, bending it in right angles. He then held the wine cork by his flies and with a great flourish took out his willy and drove the right-angled fork prong through his foreskin and into the wine cork 'anvil'. He stood up 'no hands' to prove to all it was no optical illusion.

'That satisfy yer?' he leered, at the transfixed Canadians.

Everybody's mouth opened and eyes widened. Then all the sappers let out the most spontaneous, ribald cheer I have ever heard, laughing at the unexpected solution to a potentially awkward stand-off.

The Canadian who had raised the challenge turned green and swallowed hard. As one man, he and his table wisely got up and left. After the incident involving the cork, the fork & the pork, the party continued. Believe me, being a little older and wiser I left too, but at a discrete time interval after the Canadians.

The next day, having had a better night's sleep than most, I hired a bike and set off to explore the Croatian coast. Not for me the opportunity to get drunk and let off steam that way. I needed time out away from the madding crowd to have time with the Lord and just be.

The coastal road away from the little town was a far cry from the claustrophobia of our base in Bosnia. It was even a far cry from the convivial noise of the R&R base town square.

It was just what I needed. I called in at the Krka Falls, a waterfall national park where I chatted to a Croatian soldier home on leave. He spoke German and so did I, although I did not need to be a skilled linguist to understand his hatred for the Serbs. I remember thinking 'Angry young man!' and that he would not be my first choice for a peacekeeper.

I cycled on to Sibenik, a lovely Croatian old stone town on the coast, trying to adjust back to normal after the stresses of the conflict. Though my attempt to visit the cathedral was barred by a very poker-faced priest who said I was inappropriately dressed!

It was just good to cover some miles, and talk to the Lord, and simply unwind.

I cycled on to another town, but there were not many people around and quite a lot of soldiers, which was odd. The town itself was seriously war damaged, with more sandbags than glass in the windows. Near the town centre was a bridge over the river; being the Former Republic of Yugoslavia at that time, it was the *remains* of a bridge. I parked the bike and walked up to the edge, where the bridge deck was cut away in front of me. It was like being on the set of an apocalypse movie, standing on the edge of a demolished road bridge in a ruined town, and I could peer down at the boiling river water below. Professional interest as a sapper meant I was interested in how the bridge had been demolished, where they had placed the explosive charges, what sized gap had it created, etc, etc, etc...

At this point I became aware that I was not the only one on the bridge. I was now flanked by two bleak looking Croat policemen. They wanted to know who I was. My Serbo-Croat did not work, so they tried German, which did. Well, honesty is the best policy, so I told them I was a UN peacekeeper from the UK on R&R. They did not believe me, so I told them again. It was useful to be able to speak German.

They still did not believe me and their body language, size and possession of firearms indicated to me they were possibly thinking of concluding the interview, either with some target practice with me as the target or by simply lobbing me off the bridge into the foaming water below.

This interview was not going my way and once again I knew to not show fear. And once again I had a prompting from the Holy Spirit at just the right time. And the prompting was to talk about football. So, I asked one of them if he supported Manchester United. Well, it turned out he did!

Now I knew nothing about Manchester United, but many of my sappers knew a lot about it and did not shut up about it either, so I had listened to them wax lyrical about their favourite subject. A lot. And I even remembered some of it.

Thus, the Lord enabled me to get some kind of Manchester United conversation going, in German, to ease the situation. I felt a bit of a hypocrite; I am no football fan and hardly follow the sport. However, neither had I any plans to leave the bridge and enter the river in an unplanned manner, or indeed become in any way inconvenient to these two gentlemen. I allowed myself to be very interested in football.

They smiled, shook my hand and laughed. Well, of course I could leave, and why not. They indicated that the road I had cycled in on was the way I should leave this fine town and the conversation became more relaxed.

It transpired that they had only stopped me because to them I was an unknown civilian in a town which was suddenly in the front line of the civil war. This followed a rapid advance by the Serbs to within about three miles of where we were now standing. My innocent bridge inspection made the policemen doubly curious and they had wondered if I were a spy. I was much more convincing as a British peacekeeper, out for a bike ride, who should have checked how the war was going before pedalling up the coast.

NEHEMIAH IN THE NINETIES

I did not hang around for them to change their mind, but leapt onto my bike, pedalled swiftly away to safety, and put a good distance between myself and the war.

* * * * *

Going home on leave from an operational tour like Bosnia is a unique experience. I realise that countless servicemen and servicewomen have done it; since the 'war on terror', many more have gone home on leave from an intense operational situation to the relative calm of the UK. It is quite a culture shock.

Bosnia probably does not compare to operations in Iraq or Afghanistan, so I will not try to make common cause here. But I will briefly describe it, because there will be readers who do not have any idea what a shock it is to leave an operational tour with the Army and have two weeks off in the middle. The challenge is having to assimilate into UK life for a fortnight and then re-adjust back to the tempo of the operational environment which you left just two weeks previously.

Landing in the UK after R&R was surreal. I had been working flat out in a war zone and suddenly I was home, with my parents, sitting in the garden and the cricket was on! I remember calling in for a drink in a pub with my Dad, whereupon some joker let off some fireworks outside. I nearly jumped through the window. People back home can have little idea of what it is like 'out there'. That is not their fault, but it helps if there is some awareness of this gap. This is one reason why I am describing it.

I had not appreciated how keyed up and wound up I was because of being in Bosnia, leading soldiers and mindful of potential threat to life and limb (theirs and mine). In fairness, my family was very good about this and gave me a lot of space, but many people with no experience of the military have no idea of this.

This can cause tensions when they meet someone back from a warzone, who is trying hard to readjust. Everyone is different in how they readjust, but the first step is in realising that this space is needed.

I remember attending a friend's wedding a day or so before I returned to Bosnia. It was a lovely event, with a reception in a country house, the sun shone and all in all it was a 'Forever England' type of day. It was a million miles from the simmering, fractured nation to which I was returning. I remember the pastor who married the couple asked for a few moments of my time during a gap in the wedding photos. He made a sincere effort to understand the transition I had made in coming home and was about to make in going back to Bosnia. I greatly appreciated his thoughtfulness as a non-military person trying to understand. He simply listened respectfully and did not try to summarise my thoughts and feelings for me. I was grateful then, and still am.

* * * * *

I knew I only had six weeks or so to 'push' before the end of the tour in Bosnia for the squadron and my Field Troop. Then we would return to our base in Germany. This helped me psychologically to deal with being on leave and prepare for the end of the tour.

It was easier than I thought to get back into the routine 'swing' of operations, but a military unit like a sapper field squadron is a well-oiled machine (in every sense of the word!). So it was not hard to understand that as a soldier I must keep in step with the organisation *to* which I was responsible (i.e. the squadron), whilst as an officer ensuring the organisation *for* which I was responsible (i.e. the Field Troop) was also in step. In other words, business as usual!

Adjusting to operational tempo again, whilst pushing ahead with a project where there is constant time pressure, is an interesting art that I did not find easy. I will describe how I fared in the next chapter.

Chapter 16 - Home and Well

Psalm 40: 1-3:

'I waited patiently for the Lord; he turned to me and heard my cry. He lifted me out of the slimy pit, out of the mud and mire; he set my feet on a rock and gave me a firm place to stand. He put a new song in my mouth, a hymn of praise to our God. Many will see and fear the Lord and put their trust in him.'

We all knew that we were well past the half-way mark of our operational tour and would be heading back to Germany soon.

Much of the remaining six weeks was spent chasing seemingly non-existent supplies from the UN for the bridge site and keeping on top of changing priorities regarding task lists and activities. After the intense build-up of the overbridge and the anticipated progress of the underbridge, the stop-start reality of being subject to the UN supply chain was a bit of an anti-climax.

So, I was visiting the bridge site virtually every day, chasing stores, checking that the formwork and shuttering was ready for the concrete pour, verifying that the concrete pads were in the right place, chasing stores again and generally keeping very busy. However, the sense of achievement was muted compared to building the overbridge, because often the resources and stores were delayed. This meant that there was a lot of rescheduling to keep working with what we had, rather than what we needed.

When it came to handing over to the next sapper Field Troop to take its turn after us, I found it hard to conceal my disappointment that we had not been able to finish the bridge. Alas, no frowning or grinding of teeth or stamping feet on my part would speed up the delivery of UN stores. I had to accept that we would not be the ones finishing what we had started.

Sappers also like to be kept busy because it makes the days pass quicker. I found sappers can make the best of any situation, and six months in Bosnia was quite a situation. Yet to a man they were all looking forward to the end of the operational tour. Half a year is long enough.

Don't get me wrong, the Field Troop and I were not struggling for things to do; there were always pieces of road needing repair, or more fortification works, or a generator needing to be maintained. General Montgomery was still right when he observed that there were 'never enough sappers' in a theatre of operations like Bosnia. There is always more to be done, or what has already been done needs to be improved. Sadly, there were no more helicopter landing site recces to do.

By now, the tempo was starting to change and other Royal Engineer units were deploying to Bosnia, but not with the UN. The Dayton Accord was beginning to bite and NATO was getting involved with peace support operations to make regional stability a reality. Many of my colleagues deployed to Bosnia as part of that operation.

Bosnia had been a tough, yet very fulfilling tour of duty. The Lord had protected me in line with the Word He had given me through Psalm 91 and my trust in Him had been repaid many, many times over. He not only looked after me, He prospered me. I know fellow sapper officers who were blown up by mines in Bosnia, yet I did not receive a scratch or injury during my time there. I have since visited the World War One battlefields, which are a stark reminder of how many do not return from the combat zone. I had got off very lightly. Neither did I have to fire a weapon in anger, and many years on I am glad I was not required to take life, nor order my soldiers to do so. But I would have been prepared to and under similar circumstances, I still would.

My prosperity in Bosnia is also linked to the fact that a lot of people were praying for me during the tour of duty. It was not just the OCU prayer group, but other Christians I knew who were aware that accidents and incidents can happen in a lively place like Bosnia. Every Christian has an enemy who prowls like a roaring lion wanting to kill and destroy. This prayer support was vital to my well-being and success; I shudder to think of the potential disasters that may have occurred without it. Prayer works.

As I wrote up my handover notes for the next Royal Engineers Troop Commander who was taking over from me, I reflected on what I had seen and experienced in Bosnia.

I penned a few lines on Operation Grapple to capture the moment in time. The first six lines are an acrostic, which spell 'Bosnia'. It shows some of the wider frustrations of which I was aware. These include the French government's perceived involvement in Sarajevo and the general feeling amongst the UK military that we were working flat out to solve an intractable problem. And throughout the six months, I could never ignore how the war had made life so miserable for the ordinary Bosnian people. The poem is copied below, with a couple of slight subsequent edits to simplify one or two very much 'in' jokes at the time of writing:

Operation Grapple

Bosnia in the nineties – the most desolate of places,
Of world renown for cruelty between its warring races,
Serb versus Croat and crescent versus cross,
No faction yet the winner in this war of mutual loss,
Ignore the fact each army thinks that 'God won't let us lose',
As history is the reason and religion the excuse.

* * *

The hatred in the region lies just beneath the crust,
Stemming from a civil war of neighbourly mistrust.
Every few kilometres a devastated village,
'Ethnic Cleansing,' but a modern phrase for systematic pillage.

The tinderbox of Europe is a good name for this land,
Sarajevo 1914 and the death of Ferdinand,
And the trials the French are facing are surely nothing new,
Do they know that Sarajevo is now twinned with Dien Bien Phu?

And ethnic cleansing no surprise to this divided realm,
Utashas murdered Chetniks with Hitler at the helm,
And in the middle ages, when Ottoman held sway,
Persecution of the infidel was normal in their day.

The seeds of ethnic conflict have since been sown elsewhere,
And Western Serbs taste bitter fruit of Bosnian warfare.
So the Krajinians are defeated now – a lesson for its teacher,
'Hit us and we will hit you back'...like Zepa and Sebrinica.

Yugoslavia in Tito's time a distant memory,
Can a Bosnian today define 'Racial Equality'?
If your hometown is reminiscent of Berlin in forty-five,
And you are the only member of your family left alive.

Would you settle for a cease-fire, ratified and sealed?
When the pastures where once you played are one unmarked minefield.
Grateful to the UN in their luxurious Land Cruisers?
When you know that in this conflict it's the Bosnians who are losers.

You drive the dirt track highways, strewn with Bosnia litter,
See black-toothed women staring back, do you wonder that they're bitter?
They know our time will soon be up, we'll soon be gone – no fear!
Until it's our turn on the tour plot, and we're here again next year.

And then it was time to go home…

After the intensity of the tour of duty, our departure from Bosnia felt surreal to me. You always know the day will come, but for so much of the tour it seems a million miles away and into the next century. And when the day came there was nothing else to do but board the transport back to Split (hoping the local police were still not trying to solve the mystery of a strange pub brawl a few months earlier) and from there, fly back to Germany. Suddenly, it really was all over.

And then we were back in Germany. The squadron was back into a similar 'post operational tour' state of flux as I remembered all too clearly when first I joined it. People needed to get away on leave, on career courses, on training, and the postings out began.

For my post-tour leave, I visited Eastern Europe again, this time with the Support Troop Commander with whom I had become very good friends. We went by rail to Poland, then south to Hungary.

He was settling in his mind what to do for the rest of his life and like a sensible bloke, he knew that relationships were important. We discussed this a lot, both in Bosnia and on leave. It was when we got to Budapest, drinking coffee on the hillside on the 'Buda' half of the Danube Bank that he concluded that he wanted to marry his long-term girlfriend. It was a sensible course of action and so he set off back to the UK to pop the question, leaving me smiling at being thus abandoned. Relationships are important.

I continued through Hungary, either hitch-hiking or by rail, to get a feel for a very hospitable and pleasant nation, to which I hope to return.

I passed my Captain's exam and with that out of the way, I soon found it was my turn to be posted to another unit, to do a different job. This time I was to go to the Royal Engineers Apprentice Training Wing, where the 16/18-year-old recruits to the sappers began their military training. Given that so many of my brighter sappers in the Field Troop had been apprentices themselves, I was really looking forward to having a hand in shaping the raw material of tomorrow's Royal Engineers.

It meant a return to the UK, and re-integration with life in Britain. It meant no more driving on the wrong side of the road and better prospects for church and fellowship. But I was a Captain now and very conscious of how the Lord had blessed me so much in the space of two years. I left Germany a very different person to the somewhat apprehensive guy who had first shown up at the squadron and inspected his first Field

Troop. My self-confidence had grown, but my confidence in the Lord had grown even more.

I had discovered that I thrived in His call on my life and I even found I was reasonably good at civil engineering in the combat zone. Yet the Lord was the one that gifted me. At the beginning of this book I said:

'Not every element of soldiering and being an army officer came naturally to me, but I worship a supernatural God and that changed everything.'

It is true. He had called me and confirmed that calling. And where the Lord calls, He also equips and enables. The Lord rescued me from much that could have overwhelmed or destroyed me. He also gave me the means to deal with it, as opposed to just lifting me out of situations altogether. Psalm 40:1-3 at the beginning of this final chapter exemplifies this rescuing, but also being in a firm place to stand and declare His goodness for others to see His goodness. How often do our prayers in adversity follow the theme 'Get me out of here!', instead of 'Get me through this,' or, better still, 'Enable me to triumph here for your Name's sake, O Lord and may You receive all the glory!'?

The Lord had called me to the army, and He had not just enabled me to get by, He had enabled me to flourish. Our God is a 'how much more' God, rather than a 'just enough' God. His grace is indeed sufficient, but He always gives us more. If nothing else, it means we have extra to give away.

I am always struck by how in the Gospels, Jesus lives, walks, eats and breathes life in the Holy Spirit during his three years ministering before His crucifixion. He gets His hands dirty. Yet He regularly spent time alone with His Father. My testimony is that the Lord blessed me when I spent time with Him. It didn't insulate me from the effects of the rough and tumble of a fallen world (and it didn't insulate Jesus, either), but I found the strength in the Lord to do what I had to do.

Writing this makes me ask the question 'Am I still spending enough time with Him?'

It remains a good question, for any Christian.

In the Book of James, it says we are to:

> '*Consider it pure joy, when we face trials of all kinds…*'

I wish we did not have to face trials, but alas we do because we are ambassadors for Jesus to a fallen world and like Him we have to get our hands dirty from time to time. What I cannot stress enough is that the Lord is faithful, he stays with us and acts on our behalf. It may not feel like it, but He does not allow us to be tested beyond what we can endure, and His purpose is for us to be like Him, rather than have a life of convenience. The Lord always has a higher plan for us than just our circumstances.

I have learned that the Lord looks after those who love Him and that by trusting Him, He had looked after me, protected me and blessed me beyond all my expectations. The challenge many of us face is remembering His faithfulness in the previous trial when we are going through the current trial. No, I have not yet fully cracked that one, either!

Romans 14:17 says:

> '*For the kingdom of God is not a matter of eating and drinking, but of righteousness, peace and joy in the Holy Spirit.*'

If I knew then what I know now about the Lord's love and plan for my life I would have enjoyed it so much more. I continue to learn that my life is hidden with Christ and is therefore an adventure and not an ordeal. Sometimes it can feel like an ordeal and sometimes these negative feelings can go on a long time. Yet I am increasingly learning that embracing negative feelings risks eclipsing the Lord's joy, peace and righteousness that is ours by divine right in Christ. We must live by what the Lord says, not by how we feel. Matthew 4:4 says:

> *'Jesus answered, 'It is written: 'Man shall not live on bread alone, but on every word that comes from the mouth of God.'*

God's favour is equally shared among His children and that includes you and me; it is ours by divine right.

The path and the plan that the Lord had and has for me was right for me. His path and plan for you is right for you.

This whole book it is written as an encouragement and an exhortation to follow His plan for *your life*. His plan for you is unique to you. No one else can live His plan for your life but you.

The purpose of this book is to encourage Christians to realise that the Lord really is with them and that His kindness means that you cannot help but prosper when the Lord is in your life. Yes, bad stuff can still happen, and I wish it didn't. But the Lord is with us in the valley as well as on the mountain top. I need regular reminding of this fact because it is too easy to allow circumstances and feelings to rob you of the reality of the Lord's presence and power.

The daily discipline of reading the Bible, speaking in tongues and engaging with the Lord in praise, worship and prayer is an essential habit of a prosperous and contented Christian. It is not a guarantee that bad things won't happen, but it really helps to deal with them if they do. And when they don't, your closeness with the Lord means the good times become even better.

* * * * *

Meanwhile, fresh challenges awaited back in the UK and in the Royal Engineers Apprentice Training Wing. Further opportunities were to come where the Lord blessed me, prospered me and sometimes simply delivered me from the entertaining consequences of my own stupidity…again!

And God willing, I will also write about those one day.

Glossary - British Army and Royal Engineer terms

A Brief Guide to British Army and Royal Engineers Ranks and Responsibilities

Officers:	Responsibility:
General	Army/Division
Brigadier	Brigade (three/four battalions or battlegroups)
Colonel	Senior Staff Officer
Lieutenant Colonel	Battle Group or Regimental Commanding Officer (CO), with three/four squadrons
Major	Squadron Commander, known as Officer Commanding (OC), with three/four Troops
Captain	Can be a junior Staff Officer, OC or even a Senior Field Troop Commander
Lieutenant	Field Troop Commander, of 30-40 sappers
Second Lieutenant	Field Troop Commander, of 30-40 sappers

Non-Commissioned Officers and Soldiers:	Responsibility:
Warrant Officer First Class (WO1)	Regimental Sergeant Major (RSM), the Commanding Officer's right-hand man in regimental discipline
Warrant Officer Second Class (WO2)	Squadron Sergeant Major (SSM), the OC's right-hand man in squadron discipline.

Staff Sergeant (Infantry: Colour Sergeant)	The 'Troop Staffy', the Field Troop Commander's right-hand man
Sergeant	Often a reconnaissance role in the Royal Engineers
Corporal	Commands a section of 8-10 sappers
Lance Corporal	Deputy section commander or storeman
Private	This rank is called a Sapper in the Royal Engineers. In short, they are generally the ones tasked with doing the work!

A Brief Guide to British Army Vocabulary and 'Jargon'

Adjutant	A regimental position occupied by a seasoned Captain, the adjutant is primarily responsible for executive support for the CO and is generally oversees officer discipline on behalf of the CO. The adjutant works closely with the RSM to maintain all ranks discipline across the regiment. It is a key regimental role.
Batsims	Short for 'battlefield simulations.' These are small explosive charges used to simulate explosions during battle in order to make training more effective. Design of these appropriate charges can reproduce the sound of rifle fire, or an artillery barrage, or a rocket attack, or other such scenario. Batsims are a Royal Engineer speciality.
Cavalry	In the British Army, many of its armoured (tank) regiments are still referred to as 'Cavalry', or 'Cav', reflecting their equestrian origins. Many 'Cavalry' regiments still maintain their own stables and many of their officers are accomplished horse riders. They are very good at going to war in Challenger tanks, too.

Equipment Bridge	A bridge built by hand by sappers of the Royal Engineers, mainly from prefabricated metal pieces that are assembled in a sequential way, rather like Meccano. Bailey Bridge, as used in World War 2, is the most famous example. The size of gap determines how many segments are required and the bridge is built a repetitive section at a time, which means that they are in planning terms straightforward to build. Building them quickly is a very physical task in which Royal Engineers take great pride. Troop Commanders plan the build, greatly assisted by the Troop Staff Sergeant, who controls the build. The Field Sections do the building – the hard graft.
Field Troop and Field Section	The correct name for a 'platoon' of Royal Engineers, roughly thirty in size, commanded by a lieutenant with a staff sergeant as right-hand man. The Field Troop contains three to four Field Sections of about eight men, each commanded by a corporal. The Field Troop also has a driver/signaller, plus a stores corporal, usually a lance corporal.
GPMG	General Purpose Machine Gun, a standard medium machine gun throughout the British Army, firing lots of 7.62mm bullets as and when required.
Infantry	Soldiers who traditionally go to war on foot. In the British army, it is the units who are expected to bear the brunt of the actual fighting and hold/win/defend the ground. British infantry has a strong fighting tradition going back many centuries.
JNCO	Junior Non-Commissioned Officer. Either a corporal or a lance corporal, with a corporal often doing a role such as field section commanding, and the lance corporal acting as Field Section Second in Command, or a specialist such as a storeman or key asset operator.

Light Wheel Tractor	A very versatile JCB-type tractor, with forks/bucket in the front and a 'back-acter' or excavator at the back. A useful workhorse for a range of sapper tasks, either in its own right or in support of a Field Section.
MSR	Main Supply Route. In Bosnia, these are the routes used by articulated lorries which comprise the essential convoys which delivered the humanitarian aid to people in central Bosnia. Keeping these open was one of the key tasks of the Royal Engineers on Operation 'Grapple'.
Officers' Mess	This is where all the single (or married, unaccompanied) officers live in a regiment. During my commissioned army service, as a single man I lived in officers' messes when in barracks. The officers' mess has an ante-room, where officers can socialise, a bar and dining area. They operated (and probably do still operate) by a strict set of rules. For example, wearing a suit, or jacket and tie for dinner at a set time. Sitting down together for the evening meal was the norm and sometimes inconvenient, but it made for good team building amongst regimental officers. Officers were expected to be hospitable to guests and not misbehave.
Orbat	This is short for 'order of battle' and it describes how a unit breaks down into its component parts in an operational situation to accomplish its tasks. There is significant flexibility in Royal Engineer field troops to vary the distribution of its Field Sections, based on what tasks there are. This is even truer in the case of a field squadron, which has more assets such as command vehicles, plant vehicles and engineer stores, to arrange. Orbat often describes the formation of an advancing unit, too.

Padre	A military term for an army chaplain. Often ordained ministers from the Anglican, Roman Catholic, Methodist and occasional Baptist denominations. I believe there are also Jewish and Moslem Padres in the forces today. The Padres in the army have officer rank but are not expected to command. They do not carry weapons and are classed as non-combatants. Their role is that of pastoral care: spiritual support, both publicly and privately, at every level of the army and moral guidance through formal teaching, counsel, and personal example. Army chaplains, together with other commissioned non-combatants like army doctors and nurses, do a special six-week commissioning course at Sandhurst which the rest of the army irreverently calls the 'Vicars and Tarts Course'.
QMSI	Quartermaster Sergeant Instructor. A Warrant Officer Class Two (see 'ranks' and 'SNCO') rank, which is next up from Staff Sergeant. It means that the experience of a Royal Engineers staff sergeant is then utilised in a training post. Most regiments in both the regular army and TA have QMSIs, to raise the standards of training in units across the army.
Regular Army	The UK's full time, professional army. The UK does not have National Service or conscription, so national defence is undertaken by career soldiers and officers. A recruit could 'sign-on' for at least three years and have the potential for a career spanning two-three decades.
REME	Royal Electrical and Mechanical Engineers (REME). At army unit level, REME supplies mechanical and electrical support to the front-line army units such as infantry, cavalry, artillery, Royal Engineers and air corps. An engineer regiment would have a significant REME workshop attached to it to fix and repair its large amount of mechanical and electrical vehicles and equipment.

Sapper	A private soldier in the Royal Engineers, as well as a term to describe a military engineer, especially in the British Army. The term comes from the sap trench, a zig zag trench dug by besiegers towards the fortification or town being besieged so that the besiegers cannot fire directly into the trench – its zig zag means it always has a rampart facing the enemy protecting the besieging troops. In the Royal Engineers, each sapper is a trained infantryman, as well as a combat engineer (trained in bridging, mine work, demolitions, water supply, armoured warfare, signals, etc.) and a tradesman (brick layer, or a carpenter, or a surveyor, or an electrician, etc.). The British Army refers to anyone from the Royal Engineers as a 'sapper'. I was often summoned into the presence of senior, non-Royal Engineer officers with the cry 'Ah, Sapper, come over here!'
Saxon	A wheeled Armoured Personnel Carrier used by the British Army during the 'Cold War' and still in use in reasonable numbers during the nineties. It was like a standard army truck, but with metal protection for passengers and crew of about ten to twelve soldiers, or a Field Section. We had one available to the Field Troop in Bosnia, so the Field Section working the greatest distance from base used it. This was because in an emergency it offered some protection from bullets and shell fragments, as well as a fighting platform that our other 'soft-skin' vehicles (Land Rovers and army trucks) could not; and back-up may have taken a while to arrive.

SNCO	Senior Non-Commissioned Officer. This means sergeants, staff sergeants and warrant officers (such as sergeant majors [see 'ranks and responsibilities] and QMSIs). They are experienced sappers and any new Troop Commander does well to listen to their advice, because they have years of experience that a junior officer, despite his/her training, does not.
Spartan	A light tank, or Combat Vehicle Reconnaissance (Tracked) [CVR (T)] used by Royal Engineer Commanders such as officers and SNCOs on exercise and on operations. It has a driver and a commander. It carries a single GPMG as armament.
Territorial Army (TA)	The name for the UK's part-time army in use during the 90s. Made up of civilians who committed at least two weeks and two weekends to military training a year (and many committed considerably more than that). Its purpose in the nineties was to provide reinforcements for the regular army, though today it is designed to be more closely integrated with the regular army. It is now called the Army Reserve and its role and application has altered.
Warrior Armoured Fighting Vehicle (AFV)	The standard British Army infantry fighting vehicle. It looked like a tank, carried 8-10 soldiers and had a crew of two. It also carried a 30mm Rarden cannon and 'chain gun', which provided very useful firepower. The Warrior was extremely fast and as far as I could tell, was very popular with its users.
432	An armoured personnel carrier, or basically a metal box on tracks that transports a section of sappers. It was also called a 'Pack' by its crews, for some obscure reason. It had been in service for years.

A Brief Guide to the Role of the Royal Engineers

When I joined, the Royal Engineers led in at least the following combat engineering tasks (plus other tasks not listed) below:

- Bridge construction.
- Mine warfare, especially mine clearance.
- Field fortifications (e.g. anti-tank obstacles and barbed wire).
- Water supply.
- Battlefield construction and earth moving.
- General construction tasks (e.g. hospitals in the field).
- Airfield Damage Repair (e.g. keeping bombed airfields operational).
- Watermanship (e.g. boat handling in fresh or inshore water).
- Demolitions (e.g. destroying bridges so the enemy cannot use them).
- Bomb disposal (e.g. unexploded shells).
- Combat Diving (e.g. underwater inspection of foundations).
- Survey work (e.g. Map making).

In the nineties, the Royal Engineers also committed a squadron to both the Royal Marines and the Parachute Brigade. There was also a Regiment of Ghurkha Engineers to support the Brigade of Ghurkhas, which I had already visited in Hong Kong.

But what did a normal Mechanised Engineer Regiment, like the one I eventually joined in Germany, look like?

In simple terms, it was a unit of between 450 and 650 soldiers, commanded by a Lieutenant Colonel, who was known as the Commanding Officer, or CO. The CO was assisted by the Regimental Sergeant Major, or RSM. Both CO and RSM often had about twenty years' service each and were the senior officer and soldier respectively of the regiment. The regimental second in command was a senior major and there was a quartermaster, also a major who was often a commissioned soldier, perhaps a former RSM. These 'Late Entry Officers,' who had risen through the ranks, were great characters, often quite formidable, who possessed immense experience and were good at sharing it. They were often known as 're-treads'.

The regiment was then divided into three or four Squadrons (the equivalent of a company in an infantry unit) of between 100 and 150 soldiers. There was also a small Headquarters element, which was geared towards the smooth running of the regiment and could provide engineer support to an army brigade or division.

Each Squadron was commanded by a major, known as the Officer Commanding, or OC. The OC was assisted by the Squadron Sergeant Major, or SSM. Both OC and SSM often had about ten to fifteen years' service each and were the senior officer and soldier respectively of the squadron.

My experience was limited to field squadrons, so I will not describe an armoured engineer squadron which had tanks which carried either carrying folding bridges, or bundles of poles called 'fascines' and other such clunky gadgets.

A field squadron was divided up into troops (the equivalent of a platoon in the infantry). There was a small 'Echelon Troop', which was usually commanded by a captain who had been a soldier. His next step would be that of the regimental quartermaster and he was a Late Entry Officer. Echelon Troop generally looked after communications, logistics and stores. Royal Engineers have a very distinct need for stores that the rest of the army does not require, ranging from construction equipment, to mines, to explosive charges, to the components needed for a 240-foot equipment bridge; Echelon Troop were important.

There was also a Support Troop, often commanded by a senior Lieutenant. Support Troop contained the plant machinery such as diggers & excavators which are crucial in helping a field squadron in moving earth and other battlefield construction tasks. These tasks could be that of digging tank traps for enemy tanks, or making a basic road to enable supplies to be brought up to army units.

Last, but not least, were usually three Field Troops. Each Troop was commanded by a Second Lieutenant or Lieutenant, with a Staff Sergeant to assist. In reality, the Staff Sergeant did considerably more than assist, as this book will show.

The Field Troop consisted of approximately 30 Royal Engineers. The Troop Commander and Staff Sergeant each had a driver (for their respective armoured vehicle, not as a free taxi) and a signaller. There was often a Troop Storeman, who was responsible for all the kit a Field Troop would require.

The remaining 25 or so soldiers were divided into three sections, each commanded by a Corporal and assisted by a Lance Corporal. During peace time, many soldiers were away on leave, or courses, refresher training and other duties so often required of Royal Engineers so the numbers in barracks could drop to single figures. But on operations, the expectation was to deploy at full strength. Less leave and fewer courses then!

In case you are interested, the role of a Sergeant could vary from squadron to squadron. Sometimes, they were part of the field troops and helped the Staff Sergeant, often with running the stores. More often, they were kept busy with Squadron headquarters; on exercise and operations, they would take on a reconnaissance (recce) role to provide engineer intelligence about the battlefield. This enabled the army commanders to understand the ground on which they were fighting or about to fight, so that they could deploy their forces more effectively. Which meant field troop commanders had to work harder!

This is because in wartime, the role of the Troop Commander is to command the Field Troop and the role of the Troop Staff Sergeant is to control the Field Troop.

In simple terms, it is the role of the Troop Commander to plan and recce the next task, be it a bridge, a minefield or demolitions for example. Meanwhile, the Troop Staff Sergeant would organise the Field Troop in readiness for the Troop Commander's orders, which would be a formal briefing for how the Troop would successfully complete the next task. On receipt of these orders the Troop Staff Sergeant would then get the Field Troop on task and doing it. Once the task was started, the Field Troop Commander would then go and recce the next task and the whole cycle would begin again.

Now each sapper is trained as a basic infantryman, so is a capable soldier who can use his rifle; a sapper is first and foremost a soldier. In addition, a sapper is trained as a combat engineer and so is proficient in many, if not all, of the combat engineer skills that I listed previously. And on top of this, a sapper is also a trained tradesman. Across the Royal Engineers, these would include armoured engineers to operate the 'bridge-laying' tanks, as well as bomb disposal, and military plant operators. Within a field troop, these trades would include:

- Plumber
- Electrician
- Bricklayer
- Painter and Finisher
- Surveyor
- Metal worker
- Carpenter

- Welder
- HGV Driver
- Fitter (for key engineering equipment)

So, a sapper is a soldier, a combat engineer and a tradesman. I remember being incredibly impressed when I first learned this and years later, I still am. If it helps to put this into context, I remember being told that a single engineer Field Troop should have all the skills necessary to build a permanent functioning army field hospital from scratch. No doubt Nehemiah needed more than just bricklayers in his team that rebuilt Jerusalem's wall.

Obviously, considerable sapper staff work goes into ensuring that the skills are evenly spread across the Field Troops; a section made up of only electricians is no good at just laying foundations…

A sapper Field Troop Commander had a well-trained, talented workforce to lead; these sappers were no fools, were extremely well motivated and expected high standards from themselves and those who led them.

www.ingramcontent.com/pod-product-compliance
Lightning Source LLC
LaVergne TN
LVHW041248080426
835510LV00009B/644